Pornography, Obscenity & The Law

Pornography, Obscenity & The Law

Edited by Lester A. Sobel

Contributing writers: Seth Abraham, Raymond Hill,
Stephen Orlofsky, Lauren Sass

Facts On File
119 West 57th Street, New York, N.Y. 10019

Pornography, Obscenity & The Law

77101

Library of Congress Cataloging in Publication Data

Main entry under title:

Pornography, obscenity & the law.

1. Obscenity (Law)—United Studies.
I. Sobel, Lester A. II. Facts on File, inc., New York.
KF9444.P67   345'.73'0274   79-882
ISBN 0-87196-299-3

9 8 7 6 5 4 3 2 1
PRINTED IN THE UNITED STATES OF AMERICA

Contents

Pornography & Obscenity in America

The 'Age of Porn'

A MERICA "IS DEEP INTO the Age of Porn," reports the news magazine *Time*. "There can be little doubt that America is entrenched in pornography," Representative Lee H. Hamilton (D, Ind.) asserts in his June 29, 1977 news letter to his constituents.

For most Americans, there is no need for *Time* or Congressman Hamilton to inform them of the situation. They need only walk the downtown streets of their own cities to see the massage parlors, topless bars and strip joints vie for attention with "news" stands crowded with sexually oriented magazines, "adult" book stores displaying similar wares and hawking other pornographic lures and theaters exhibiting X-rated (or unrated) motion pictures and "live sex acts."

Many Americans have already noted the changes over the past two decades that have brought pornography up from under the counters of a few furtive newspaper vendors to favored positions in many news stalls, from the clandestine productions of stag-party impresarios to the seriously reviewed offerings of the "legitimate" theater, from the sleazy depictions of sex adventures filmed hastily in somebody's apartment to fully professional cinematic works produced and directed by motion picture luminaries and with serious actors appearing in the omnipresent "nude scene."

1

Any serious attempt to deal with the subject of pornography and obscenity requires answers to several closely connected questions: What is pornographic? What is not pornographic? What is obscene? What is not obscene? How does one judge? The answers are not easy for the layman. Neither are they easy for the law. What is obscene to one lay or legal observer may be an earnest artistic effort, even an elevated work of art, to another. The criteria used by one court to test for obscenity may seem flawed, even obnoxious, to another.

Pornography is a term that at first applied to descriptions of prostitutes and prostitution. As now used, the word describes sexually "explicit" writings, still or motion pictures and similar products designed to be sexually arousing.

Obscene is a word that originally referred to "filth." As used in the theater, it often meant something that was alluded to but not shown. Obscenity still refers to something lewd, or offensive to modesty or decency. The laws against obscenity, however, apply only to the sexually obscene.

It is under the obscenity laws that pornography has been prohibited or attacked. Legal assaults on non-sexual "obscenity"—as blasphemy or portrayals of violence are sometimes described—usually take place under rules other than those created to deal with (sexual) obscenity. There is an occasional exception—the effort to curb the scatalogical; this effort sometimes takes place under the obscenity regulations.

One thing becomes immediately obvious when dealing with the subject of pornography and obscenity: as the cliche has it, "time is of the essence." What was obscene to a nineteenth century court may be innocent to a twentieth century tribunal. What was pornographic to the public of the 1940s may be inoffensive to the readers and audiences of the 1950s, 1960s or 1970s.

In 1948, when Norman Mailer's World War II novel *The Naked and the Dead* was published, readers were described as shocked (or titillated) to find the book frequently using a formerly taboo word. This term, which is extremely popular in military and other masculine circles, was consistently (and deliberately) misspelled by Mailer as "fug." This appeared to set a precedent for the acceptance of this word, with such obvious spelling, for a generally distributed novel by a standard publisher (Rinehart). Less than three years later, in 1951, James Jones' World War II novel *From Here to Eternity* used the same word with approximately equal frequency and in its full, correct, four-letter spellling. The shock (and titillation) was said to be less, and this book too received wide, general distribution by a standard publisher (Scribners). It should be added that each book achieved a measure of critical approval and that both were tremendous best-sellers. Today, the formerly taboo word is accepted without question in many books and magazines and is thought to be used almost as commonly by high-school and college girls as it is by male members of the armed forces. So are many other words formerly banned automatically from all but illicit publications.

A similar development took place in motion pictures. Before World War II, words and actions now considered inoffensive were prohibited in films. It was considered quite daring in the 1930s to have an actor use the word "damn" in the movie *Gone With the Wind*. By 1969, after a series of court rulings relaxing the restrictions on allegedly obscene films, the Swedish motion picture *I Am Curious (Yellow)* was given wide (but not uncontested) distribution in the United States despite scenes of "explicit" sex and nudity. American film makers were quick to follow with widely distributed movies depicting sex acts and nudity and including language previously prohibited as obscene. Despite complaints by religious and other anti-obscenity groups and frequent crackdowns by local authorities against allegedly pornographic films, such motion pictures are exhibited in most parts of the United States.

Books and magazines with words and photographs devoted in whole or part to sex and nudity have proliferated at a great rate since the 1950s and now are sold openly in city after city in "adult" (a standard euphemism for "pornographic") book shops, which may also purvey "kinky" paraphernalia, peep shows or "live sex performances."

By 1976 the acceptance (or toleration) of such material had mounted to something of a plateau. A political figure well known for his publicly and frequently avowed religious convictions was interviewed that year for a monthly "men's" magazine, *Playboy*, in which the most popular feature was said to be color photographs of nude young women displaying their vaginas and other parts of their bodies before the camera. Toward the end of this long and somewhat rambling interview, Jimmy Carter, shortly to be elected President of the United States, made this widely quoted remark: " . . . Christ set some almost impossible standards for us. Christ said, I tell you that anyone who looks on a woman with lust has in his heart already committed

adultery. I've looked on a lot of women with lust. I've committed adultery in my heart many times. This is something that God
recognizes I will do—and I have done it—and God forgives me
for it. But that doesn't mean that I condemn someone who not
only looks on a woman with lust but who leaves his wife and
shacks up with somebody out of wedlock. . . ."

The situation in the 1970s is described by *Time* in its April 5,
1976 edition: "Every major U.S. city has its Santa Monica
Boulevard . . . , a garish, grubby, milelong gauntlet of sex-
book stalls, theaters and 8-mm. peep shows for voyeurs, and
massage parlors and sexual encounter centers for those who
want direct action. . . ." *Time* adds, however, that "porn is
scarcely confined to such strips. . . . Ex-Prostitute Xaveria
Hollander has sold 9 million copies of her paperbacks. Some 780
American theaters, including many elegant first-run houses, rou-
tinely show X-rated movies 52 weeks a year. *Playboy* and . . .
far crasser imitators, . . . occasionally coming out with cover
shots of women masturbating, are at supermarket chains . . .
on view for millions of customers of all ages. . . . Boston
[has] . . . an anything-goes 'combat zone.'" According to
Time, "porn has mushroomed in the past decade, from a marginal underground cottage industry into an open, aggressive $2 bil-
lion-a-year, crime-ridden growth enterprise. . . ."

Congressman Hamilton tells his constituents that "most
Americans are outraged by pornography, but the Congress and
the courts are just not sure what they can or should do about it."
Repeating the findings of many press and governmental observ-
ers, Hamilton reports that pornography "has proliferated across
the land. Many newsstands are a combination of smut shop and
legitimate bookstore. Every major American city has a grubby
area for sex shops, dirty bookstores, massage parlors, prostitution, and peek shows. In Washington such an area is only a few
blocks from the White House. According to one national magazine, pornography is an ordinary topic of conversation in the
suburbs and is 'socially acceptable.'" Hamilton continues:
"For well over a century Americans have been anxious about
pornography. What is it? What effect does it have on people?
What can be done about it? The answers to these questions do
not come easily, but a feeling is strong among many Americans
that something has gone awry in our efforts to deal with it, and
the search for answers to it continues.

"The Supreme Court has held that obscenity is outside the free speech protection of the First Amendment to the United States Constitution, but the courts and the Congress have had great difficulty in determining whether certain material is obscene. In 1957 in the *Roth* case, the Supreme Court said what was sexual was not necessarily obscene and laid down the standard, 'Whether to the average person, applying contemporary community standards, the dominant theme of the material taken as a whole appears to prurient interests.'

"In 1966 the Supreme Court went still further and said that to be obscene the material had to be 'utterly without redeeming social value.' This standard, which reflected a strong reluctance by judges to allow governmental interference with free expression, opened the flood gates of pornography, and in 1973 the Court, trying to reverse the tide, modified the *Roth* case with a test of obscenity based on three elements: (1) whether 'the average person, applying contemporary community standards,' would find that the work, taken as a whole, appeals to prurient interests; (2) whether the work depicts or describes in a patently offensive way, sexual conduct specifically defined by applicable state law; and (3) whether the work taken as a whole lacks serious literary, artistic, political or scientific value.

"The court indicated that the community standards could be local and not national. Since local juries would have to decide what offended their standard of taste, and convict violators if these standards applied, this was a much easier guideline for prosecutors. No longer was it necessary for them to show that a work was utterly without redeeming social value.

"Even with that standard, pornography continued to flourish for several reasons: community standards were changing, police were arguing that pursuing perpetrators of victimless crimes represented a misuse of their limited resources, and legal procedures were cumbersome, expensive and often pointless because fines were light.

"In recent years a large number of bills have been introduced in the Congress to protect the public from pornography. The major problem continues to be the difficulty of drafting legislation that would control pornography without violating First Amendment rights, as interpreted by the Supreme Court. The most successful legislation to date is an amendment to the postal laws to stop mailing of sexually oriented commercial advertisements to persons who indicate that they do not want to receive them. This law gives citizens some measure of protection against unsolicited sex mail. Hundreds of bills introduced in the Congress to protect people from unwanted pornography seek to include a broader class of material as obscene but the problem of how to define obscenity still remains. At the moment the Congress is giving a considerable amount of attention to legislation that would prohibit the manufacture or sale of pornography using children.

"Another approach to dealing with pornography is through zoning laws to limit sex establishments—laws which have been upheld by the Supreme Court. The containment of these establishments seeks to protect the community and the individual from being confronted by offensive material. Many communities have learned that zoning can be a powerful tool in a community's arsenal to control pornography.

"I recognize the dangers of limitations on the free dissemination of ideas, and I acknowledge the necessity of proceeding with utmost caution in developing any such limitations. In a sense, pornography is one of the prices we pay for genuine, free speech. I personally, however, object to the circulation of obscene material and will support in the Congress constitutional measures to stop the flow of it. Certainly immediate steps are needed to protect minor children and the majority of Americans must be able to associate with one another without unwillingly being contaminated by pornography.

"It seems to me we can regulate where and how pornographic materials are sold. In the long run, as Justice John Paul Stevens suggested in a recent Supreme Court opinion, we must rely on 'the capacity of the free marketplace of ideas to distinguish that which is useful or beautiful from that which is ugly or worthless.' "

This book is intended as a record of the developments that produced America's "Age of Porn" and of other significant events connected with the issue of pornography and obscenity in the United States. Special emphasis is placed on the legal background of the problem, on the American constitutional guarantees with which official attacks on pornography and obscenity are sometimes said to conflict. In this respect, this volume gives particular attention to changing judicial interpretations of these guarantees. Although much of the material that follows is controversial, a conscientious effort was made to record all without bias and to make this book a balanced and accurate reference tool.

LESTER A. SOBEL

New York, N.Y.
January, 1979

The Legal Background

Early Concern With Obscenity

In the land that was to become the United States, criminal law banning obscene writings or pictures goes back at least as far as 1712, when such a ban was enacted in Massachusetts. It took more than a century, however, for an American court to render a decision on obscenity.

The first known United States court ruling on the issue was the case of *Commonwealth v. Sharpless* in 1815. Jesse Sharpless and five associates were convicted in Philadelphia of displaying for profit a picture showing "a man in an obscene, impudent, and indecent posture with a woman." Terrence G. Murphy wrote in *Censorship: Government and Obscenity* (1963) that "for more than a half-century after *Sharpless,* the issue arose seldom, but when it did, the courts generally followed the *Sharpless* precedent."

United States courts also looked to England for precedent. Before the middle of the nineteenth century, England seemed to have been indifferent to the idea of outlawing obscenity. According to Thomas I. Emerson (in *The System of Freedom of Expression,* 1970), "There is no convincing evidence that obscenity in the current sense was a common law crime in England until the enactment of Lord Campbell's Act in 1857. . . . [I]t was well into the nineteenth century, under the impact of the Victorian era, before obscenity laws played any significant part in the system of freedom of expression." It was in 1868 that Lord

Cockburn, deciding the case of *Regina v. Hicklin*, enunciated the first important guide in determining what material was obscene: ". . . I think the test of obscenity is this, whether the tendency of the matter charged as obscenity is to deprave and corrupt those whose minds are open to such immoral influences, and into whose hands a publication of this sort may fall."

Cockburn's *Hicklin* test was accepted in many American courts well into the first half of the twentieth century. It was applied in Massachusetts in such widely noted cases as the banning of Theodore Dreiser's *An American Tragedy* in 1930, Lillian Smith's *Strange Fruit* in 1945 and Erskine Caldwell's *God's Little Acre* in 1950. Yet in 1948, the less well regarded *Forever Amber* was found acceptable by the Massachusetts courts despite *Hicklin*.

The federal government's first legislative attack on pornography had taken place in the Tariff Act of 1842, which prohibited the "importation of all indecent and obscene prints, paintings, lithographs, engravings and transparancies." More than two decades passed before Congress, in 1865, passed a law banning obscene literature from the mail. It was just at about this period that a great upsurge in the business of pornography began.

In the following decade, the great crusader against pornography, Anthony Comstock, began his attack on smut. In New York in 1873, Comstock founded the Society for the Suppression of Vice. This organization and many that followed it invested considerable energy, time and devotion to the cause of stamping out salacious materials. The Comstock Act, which outlawed the mailing of any "obscene, lewd, lascivious, or filthy book, pamphlet, picture, paper, letter, writing, print or other publication of an indecent character," was enacted in 1873.

The Rev. Howard Moody wrote in the Jan. 25, 1965 issue of *Christianity and Crisis* that "the real beginning of censorship—the establishment of prudery by legal sanctions—was the work not of Puritans and Pilgrims but of nineteenth century Protestants."

Restrictions Fall, Definition Eased

Not all American judges were happy about the restrictions imposed by the *Hicklin* test for obscenity. Although Judge Learned Hand accepted them in deciding *United States v. Kennerley* in 1913, he felt constrained to add, "I hope it is not improper for me to say that the rule as laid down, however consonant it may be with mid-Victorian morals, does not seem to me to answer to the understanding and morality of the present time.''

Well before the 1948 Massachusetts decision absolving *Forever Amber*, federal and state courts had found it possible to revise or reject the *Hicklin* test. The landmark decision was rendered by Federal Judge John Woolsey in New York Dec. 6, 1933 in the case of *United States v. One Book Entitled "Ulysses."* According to Woolsey, *Ulysses* was not ''obscene within the legal definition of that word. The meaning of the word obscene as legally defined by the Courts is: tending to stir the sex impulses or to lead to sexually impure and lustful thoughts.'' ''Whether a particular book would tend to excite such impulses and thoughts must be tested by the Court's opinion as to its effect on a person with average sex instincts,'' he declared. Furthermore, he held, the book must be read and weighed ''in its entirety . . . on such a test as this'' and should not be judged on the basis of isolated excerpts, as permitted in the *Hicklin* rule.

Woolsey's decision was upheld by the Court of Appeals the following year. Judge Augustus Hand of the appellate panel, specifically rejecting the *Hicklin* test, expressed his opinion ''that the proper test of whether a given book is obscene is its dominant effect. In applying this test, relevancy of the objectionable parts to the theme, the established reputation of the work in the estimation of approved critics, if the book is modern, and the verdict of the past, if it is ancient, are persuasive pieces of evidence; for works of art are not likely to sustain a high position with no better warrant for their existence than their obscene content.''

Butler & Roth Decisions Soften Rules

The U.S. Supreme Court did not provide any real guidance in the obscenity situation until 1957, when it issued two opinions on the issue.

The first of the 1957 opinions, on a point of perhaps secondary importance, was in the case of *Butler v. Michigan*, in which the court invalidated a Michigan law that prohibited distribution to the general public of material ''containing obscene, immoral, lewd or lascivious language, or . . . pictures . . . tending to incite minors to violent or depraved or immoral acts, manifestly tending to the corruption of the morals of youth.''

The *Butler* decision was written by Justice Felix Frankfurter, who assailed the Michigan statute for "quarantining the general reading public against books not too rugged for grown men and women in order to shield juvenile innocence." The effect, he held, "is to reduce the adult population of Michigan to reading only what is fit for children."

In the second 1957 opinion, delivered in two separate cases, *Roth v. United States* and *Alberts v. California*, the Supreme Court June 27 upheld, respectively, (a) a federal statute making it illegal to mail "obscene, lewd, lascivious, or filthy" material or "other publications of an indecent character," and (b) a California law banning the publication, advertising, sale or distribution of "any obscene or indecent" material. The *Roth* decision upheld the obscenity conviction of Samuel Roth, who sold "soft-core" pornographic books and magazines in New York.

The majority opinion, written by Justice William J. Brennen Jr., stated two major principles. It held that obscenity is not a form of expression protected by the First Amendment, that it "is not within the area of constitutionally protected speech or press." Brennan, rejecting the *Hicklin* test for determining whether material is obscene, provided this new rule: it is obscene if "to the average person, applying contemporary community standards, the dominant theme of the material taken as a whole appeals to prurient interest." Brennan's opinion defined "prurient interest" as "having a tendency to excite lustful thoughts."

Explaining his rejection of the argument that the First Amendment protected obscenity, Brennan said: "All ideas having even the slightest redeeming social importance—unorthodox ideas, controversial ideas, even ideas hateful to the prevailing climate of opinion—have the full protection of the [First Amendment] guaranties, unless excludable because they encroach upon the limited area of more important interests. But implicit in the history of the First Amendment is the rejection of obscenity as utterly without redeeming social importance."

The *Roth* decision was followed widely by courts and state legislatures in defining obscenity. The New York State Legislature, for example, amended the state penal code thus: "Any material or performance is 'obscene' if (a) considered as a whole, its predominant appeal is to prurient, shameful or morbid interest in nudity, sex, excretion, sadism or masochism and (b) it goes substantially beyond customary limits of candor in describing or representing such matters, and (c) it is utterly without redeeming social value. Predominant appeal shall be judged with reference to ordinary adults unless it appears from the character of the material or the circumstances of its dissemination to be designed for children or other susceptible audience."

Three cases decided without written opinion in 1958 displayed the Supreme Court's apparent reluctance to prohibit material as obscene. In *Sunshine Book Co. v. Summerfield*, the high court reversed lower court findings that a nudist magazine was obscene. In *Times Film Corp. v. Chicago*, the court reversed an obscenity ruling against the film *Game of Love*. And it acted similarly in *One Inc. v. Olesen* in reversing such a finding against a magazine for homosexuals.

The high court provided additional guidance on the obscenity issue in 1959, in the case of *Kingsley International Pictures Corp. v. Regents of the University of the State of New York*. The New York Board of Regents, later upheld by the New York Court of Appeals, had refused to license the exhibition of the film *Lady Chatterley's Lover*. Its ground was that the movie's "whole theme is immoral" under New York state law because "that theme is the presentation of adultery as a desirable, acceptable and proper pattern of behavior." The Supreme Court reversed this decision. Justice Potter Stewart, author of the Supreme Court's majority opinion, held that the appeals court had violated the First Amendment by banning the film not because it was obscene but because of its alluring portrayal of "adultery as proper behavior." According to Stewart: "What New York has done, therefore, is to prevent the exhibition of a motion picture because that picture advocates an idea—that adultery under certain circumstances may be proper behavior. Yet the First Amendment's basic guarantee is of freedom to advocate ideas. The State, quite simply, has thus struck at the very heart of constitutionally protected liberty."

In 1964, rejecting another obscenity finding (in the case of *Jacobellis v. Ohio*), a badly split Supreme Court June 22 reversed the conviction of a Cleveland Heights, Ohio cinema theater manager, Nico Jacobellis, for exhibiting the French film *Les Amants (The Lovers)*. The film had already been shown in Washington, New York and other cities. Justice Brennan, writing for himself and for Justice Arthur Goldberg, held that material is pornographic if "to the average person, applying contemporary standards, . . . [its] dominant theme . . . taken as a whole appeals to prurient interest" and if it is "utterly without redeeming social importance."

Justices Hugo L. Black and William O. Douglas concurred on the ground that a "conviction . . . for showing a motion picture abridges freedom of the press as safeguarded by the First Amendment." Justice Stewart concurred on the ground that obscenity laws must be "constitutionally limited to hard-core pornography." He decided not to "attempt further to define the kinds of material I understand to be embraced within that shorthand description; and perhaps I could never succeed in intelligibly doing so. But I know it when I see it, and the motion picture involved in this case is not that."

Chief Justice Earl Warren and Justice Tom Clark dissented, holding that local not national standards should be used in determining such cases. Justice John Marshall Harlan, dissenting, objected to prohibiting the states "from banning any material which, taken as a whole, has been reasonably found in state judicial proceedings to treat with sex in a fundamentally offensive manner, under rationally established criteria for judging such material."

In other decisions rendered the same day but without opinion, the Supreme Court reversed Florida court decisions that Henry Miller's *Tropic of Cancer* and the book *Pleasure Was My Business* were obscene. The latter case (*Tralins v. Gertstein*) involved a book said to contain "numerous descriptions of abnormal sex acts and indecent conversation supposed to have taken place in a Florida brothel." The case of the Henry Miller book was *Grove Press v. Gerstein*. The court also found unconstitutional Kansas' seizure of 1,715 paperback books whose subject matter was largely sex.

The Supreme Court March 1, 1965 unanimously declared Maryland's methods of film censorship unconstitutional. Agreeing with a contention of Baltimore theater manager Roland Freedman that the state's law provided inadequate safeguards against undue inhibition of freedom of expression, the high court reversed a 1964 Maryland Court of Appeals decision against Freedman. (Freedman had exhibited the film *Revenge at Daybreak* in 1962 without submitting it to Maryland's Motion Picture Censor Board, as required by state law. He had subsequently been prosecuted and fined $25 although the state had not found the film obscene.) The Supreme Court's opinion, written by Justice Brennan, stated these procedural guidelines for constitutional film censorship: (1) the burden of instituting judicial proceedings should be put on the censor, not the exhibitor; (2) any exhibition restraint imposed prior to judicial proceedings must be brief; (3) there must be prompt court determination on the question of a film's obscenity.

The Supreme Court March 15, 1965, reversed a New York State Court of Appeals decision that a license could be denied for the Danish film *A Stranger Knocks* unless two scenes depicting sexual intercourse were deleted. (Under New York State law, the censor's ruling was final unless the exhibitor appealed to the state courts. The Danish film had been refused a license by the Motion Picture Division of the New York State Education Department in March 1963. This decision was sustained by the State Board of Regents June 27, 1963. The Appellate Division Nov. 21, 1963 had ruled that the exhibitor had a right to a license, but this decision was reversed by the State Court of Appeals March 26, 1964 on an appeal by the Board of Regents.) The film opened in New York March 31.

The New York Court of Appeals, the state's highest court, declared the state's movie censorship procedure "null and void" June 10, 1965. It ruled that the procedure, provided for in the Education Law, violated the 14th Amendment to the U.S. Constitution. As a result of the decision, films no longer would have to be submitted to the Board of Regents before public showing. When the U.S. Supreme Court had reversed the New York decision denying a license for the Danish film *A Stranger Knocks*, it had not declared the state procedure unconstitutional. The June 10 state court ruling was issued after the federal court returned the case to the New York courts.

Federal District Judge Henry Graven, at the end of a 10-day trial without jury in New York, Nov. 17, 1965 condemned the Swedish film *491* as obscene. He upheld the action of customs officials who had seized the film in April. The seizure was contested by *491*'s producer, Vilgot Sjoman. Graven ruled that *491* was "characterized by patent offensiveness" and was "utterly without redeeming social importance." Scenes in the film strongly implied homosexuality, sodomy, bestiality, rape and prostitution.

Written opinions were produced by the Supreme Court again in three obscenity cases in 1966. Ruling that "titillating" advertising could be used as proof that the material advertised was pornographic, the Supreme Court upheld by a 5–4 decision

March 21 the obscenity conviction of New York publisher Ralph Ginzburg for sending his magazine *Eros* and two other sexually provocative publications through the mails. The other publications were *Liaison*, a biweekly newsletter, and *The Housewife's Handbook on Selective Promiscuity*. Ginzburg had been sentenced in the lower courts to five years in prison. In a new departure in such cases, the court majority agreed with the prosecution's contention that there may be "offense in the context of the circumstances of production, sale and publicity" although "standing alone, the publications themselves might not be obscene."

In two companion cases March 21: (a) The court upheld, 6–3, the conviction and three-year prison sentence of Edward Mishkin for publishing "sadistic and masochistic" material in violation of New York's obscenity laws; (b) the court reversed, 6–3, a Massachusetts court ruling that the 18th-century novel *Memoirs of a Woman of Pleasure* (commonly known as *Fanny Hill*), by John Cleland, was obscene.

Justice Brennan, in his majority opinion in *Ginzburg v. United States*, recalled the court's obscenity standard, as stated in *Roth*: Material was obscene if it were "patently offensive" and "utterly without redeeming social value" and if "to the average persons, applying contemporary community standards, the dominant theme of the material taken as a whole appeals to prurient interest." Brennan held, however, that "consideration . . . [should be given to] the setting in which the publications were presented as an aid to determining the question of obscenity"; "in close cases" it was permissible to hold "that questionable publications are obscene in a context which brands them as obscene. . . ." Brennan viewed Ginzburg's publications against their "background of commercial exploitation of erotica solely for the sake of their prurient appeal," and in this light he found them obscene. "The 'leer of the sensualist' . . . permeats the advertising for the three publications," Brennan charged. He said that Ginzburg's "own expert agreed, correctly we think, that 'if the object [of a work] is material gain for the creator through an appeal to the sexual curiosity and appetite,' the work is pornographic."

Justices Hugo L. Black, William O. Douglas, John M. Harlan and Potter Stewart were the dissenters in *Ginzburg*. Stewart said the First Amendment "means that a man cannot be sent to prison merely for distributing publications which offend a judge's esthetic sensibilities, mine or any other's." Stewart also defined "hard-core pornography" by the use of "a description borrowed from the Solicitor General's brief": "Such materials include photographs, both still and motion picture, with no pretense of artistic value, graphically depicting acts of sexual intercourse, including various acts of sodomy and sadism, and sometimes involving several participants in scenes of orgy-like character. They also include strips of drawings in comic-book format grossly depicting similar activities in an exaggerated fashion. There are, in addition, pamphlets and booklets, sometimes with photographic illustrations, verbally describing such activities in a bizarre manner with no attempt whatsoever to afford portrayals of character or situation and with no pretense to literary value. All of this material . . . cannot conceivably be characterized as embodying communication of ideas or artistic values inviolate under the First Amendment. . . ." Black complained "that certainly after the fourteen separate opinions handed down in these three cases today no person, not even the most learned judge much less a layman, is capable of knowing in advance of an ultimate decision in his particular case by this Court whether certain material comes within the area of 'obscenity' as that term is confused by the Court today."

(Ginzburg began serving his three-year jail sentence Feb. 17, 1972 in the federal prison in Lewisburg, Pa. He was released on parole Oct. 10.)

In *Mishkin v. New York*, Mishkin's lawyer contended that the fifty books involved included both obscene works and others that were admittedly "sadistic and masochistic" but not legally obscene because they did not appeal to the prurient interest of the average person and "instead of stimulating the erotic, they disgust and sicken." Brennan's majority opinion said: "Where the material is designed for and primarily disseminated to a clearly defined deviant sexual group, rather than the public at large, the prurient-appeal requirement of the *Roth* test is satisfied if the dominant theme of the material taken as a whole appeals to the prurient interest in sex of the members of the group."

In the *Fanny Hill* case (*A Book Named "John Cleland's Memoirs of a Woman of Pleasure" v. Attorney General of Massachusetts*), Brennan said the state court's decision would have to be reversed because it admittedly found that *Fanny Hill* had "a modicum of social value." Thus it fell within the *Roth* criteria, he said. But Brennan emphasized that his decision was made solely "in the abstract" and that the obscenity decision possibly might be different if it were found that the book had been "exploited by panderers." The dissenters in this decision were Justices Harlan, Byron R. White and Tom C. Clark. The Massachusetts court had said that although "testimony may indicate this book has some minimal literary value," this "does not mean it is of any social importance." Brennan's opinion held this judgement to be in error. (The Appellate Division of the New York State Supreme Court, in a 3–2 decision Feb. 27, 1964, had adjudged *Fanny Hill* obscene and enjoined G. P. Putnam's Sons from publishing, selling and distributing it. The decision reversed an Aug. 23, 1963 ruling of Justice Arthur G. Klein, who had found it not obscene.)

The Kansas Supreme Court July 27, 1966 upheld an April 26 district court decision that the State Board of Review & Movie Censorship was unconstitutional. The decision was in a case involving Columbia Pictures, which had distributed two films without submitting them first to the three-woman board.

The Supreme Court May 8, 1967 reversed obscenity convictions in Kentucky, New York and Arkansas cases on the ground that the materials involved were not obscene under the court's current obscenity tests. The 7–2 ruling said: (1) "In none of the cases was there a claim that the statute in question reflected a specific and limited state concern for juveniles." (2) "In none was there any suggestion of an assault upon individual privacy by publication in a manner so obtrusive as to make it impossible for an unwilling individual to avoid exposure to it." (3) "And in none was there evidence of the sort of 'pandering' which the court found significant in *Ginzburg v. United States.*"

The cases involved: (a) Robert Redrup, a clerk in a New York City subway book and magazine store, who had been given a suspended sentence for selling two paperbooks entitled *Lust Pool* and *Shame Agent*; the case was *Redrup v. New York*. (b) A Paducah, Ky. bookstore owner who sold two magazines entitled *Spree* and *High Hells*. (c) The publishers of eight magazines banned in Pine Bluff, Ark. They were *Gent, Swank, Bachelor, Modern Man, Cavalcade, Gentleman, Ace* and *Sin*. Dissenting from the ruling were Justices John M. Harlan and Tom C. Clark.

The Supreme Court May 15, 1967 nullified the powers of the Oklahoma Literature Commission, established in 1957 to prohibit sale or distribution of literature it found obscene. The court affirmed a lower court ruling barring the commission from prohibiting the sale of "obscene" literature, but it reversed the lower court's finding that the Oklahoma statute that created the commission was unconstitutional.

The Supreme Court Oct. 23, 1967, reversed, 7–1, two lower court rulings that had barred from the U.S. Danish nudist magazines reportedly intended for the male homosexual market. Lawyers for book and magazine distributors in Washington had appealed on the ground that "if there are homosexual nudists, then these homosexual nudists are entitled to receive a homosexual magazine." Chief Justice Earl Warren dissented. The court Oct. 23 reversed, 8–1, the conviction of a Louisiana newsdealer who had been fined $100 for selling "girlie" magazines and nudist publications. But the court the same day let stand, 6–3, the obscenity conviction of Marcel Fort, a Miami sculptor, who had displayed for sale in his yard, 50 to 75 feet from a busy highway, six life-sized statues of males and females in erotic embraces. Justices Potter Stewart, Hugo L. Black and William O. Douglas dissented on the ground that Fort had been convicted under an "unconstitutional" Florida law. (More than two years later, over the dissents of a new chief justice, Warren E. Burger, and Justice John M. Harlan, the Supreme Court Dec. 8, 1969 overturned the conviction of Louis Carlos, a Watertown, N.Y. shopkeeper, who had been found guilty of selling obscene "girlie" magazines. In an unsigned opinion, the court cited its 1967 decision that held similar material not obscene. Burger stated that he agreed with Harlan's views that the Constitution gave less protection against states' obscenity laws than against federal statutes.)

The Supreme Court March 3, 1968 refused to overturn the Pennsylvania Supreme Court's decision that the novel *Candy* was not obscene.

Stricter Rules Valid for Children

In its first decision on censorship of children's reading matter, the Supreme Court April 22, 1968 upheld the rights of states and cities to ban sales of certain books and magazines to minors. The 6–3 ruling was on the appeal of Sam Ginsberg of New York who had been found guilty of selling "girlie" magazines to a 16-year-old boy. Justice William J. Brennan Jr. wrote the majority opinion. He said that while the literature was not obscene for adults,

"the well-being of its children is a subject within the state's constitutional power to regulate." Justices William O. Douglas,
Hugo L. Black and Abe Fortas dissented.

The New York law involved prohibited selling to minors under seventeen years of age any picture or similar representation
"which depicts nudity, sexual conduct or sado-masochistic
abuse and which is harmful to minors," or any printed matter
that contains similar material "or explicit or detailed verbal descriptions or narrative accounts of sexual excitement, sexual
conduct or sado-masochistic abuse and which, taken as a whole
is harmful to minors." The law defined "nudity," "sexual conduct," "sexual excitement," and "sado-masochistic abuse"
quite specifically. "Nudity" meant "the showing of the human
male or female genitals, pubic area or buttocks with less than a
full opaque covering, or the showing of the female breast with
less than a fully opaque covering of any portion thereof below
the top of the nipple, or the depiction of covered male genitals in
a discernibly turgid state." The expression "harmful to minors"
was linked to representations of any of the foregoing material
that "(i) predominantly appeals to the prurient, shameful or
morbid interest of minors, and (ii) is patently offensive to prevailing standards in the adult community as a whole with respect
to what is suitable material for minors, and (iii) is utterly without
redeeming social importance for minors."

Brennan asserted that the New York Legislature had decided
that the material it was prohibiting was "a basic factor in impairing the ethical and moral development of our youth and a clear
and present danger to the people of the state." Brennan called it
"very doubtful that this finding expresses an accepted scientific
fact." "But obscenity is not protected expression and may be
suppressed without a showing of the circumstances which lie behind the phrase 'clear and present danger,'" he declared, and
therefore it was necessary only that "we be able to say that it
was not irrational for the legislature to find that exposure to
material condemmned by the statute is harmful to minors."

Justice Potter Stewart, concurring, presented a rationale for
holding that the First Amendment guarantees did not always apply equally to adults and children: "The First Amendment guarantees liberty of human expression in order to preserve in our
Nation what Mr. Justice Holmes called a 'free trade in ideas.' To
that end, the Constitution protects more than just a man's freedom to say or write or publish what he wants. It secures as well

the liberty of each man to decide for himself what he will read and to what he will listen. The Constitution guarantees, in short, a society of free choice. Such a society presupposes the capacity of its members to choose. . . . I think a State may permissibly determine that, at least in some precisely delineated areas, a child—like someone in a captive audience—is not possessed of that full capacity for individual choice which is the presupposition of First Amendment guarantees. It is only upon such a premise, I should suppose, that a State may deprive children of other rights—the right to marry, for example, or the right to vote—deprivations that would be constitutionally intolerable for adults.''

In a related decision the same day, the court invalidated a Dallas city ordinance that barred children from seeing films classified as ''not suitable for young persons.'' The court ruled, 8–1, that the ordinance was too vague in its censorship standards. Justice Marshall wrote the decision and Justice Harlan dissented.

Pornography Not Illegal in Private

The right to privacy was linked to obscenity law in a 1969 case, *Stanley v. Georgia*. The Supreme Court in this case April 7 unanimously reversed the obscenity conviction of Robert Eli Stanley, in whose home in Atlanta federal and state officials, using a warrant issued in a search for bookmaking evidence, had found three reels of admittedly pornographic film. Stanley was convicted under a Georgia law against ''knowingly hav[ing] possession of obscene matter.''

Justice Thurgood Marshall, writing for himself and five other justices, held that the *Roth* and following decisions involved the ''regulation of commercial distribution of obscene material'' but did not ''foreclose an examination of the constitutional implications of a statute forbidding mere private possession of such material.'' He concluded that whatever ''may be the justifications for other statutes regulating obscenity, we do not think they reach into the privacy of one's own home. If the First Amendment means anything, it means that a State has no business telling a man, sitting alone in his own house, what books he may read or what films he may watch. Our whole constitutional heritage rebels at the thought of giving government the power to control men's minds.''

Marshall rejected the assertion that the control of the possession of obscene material was "a necessary incident to statutory schemes prohibiting distribution." On the contrary, he held, "the individual's right to read or observe what he pleases . . . is so fundamental to our scheme of individual liberty, its restriction may not be justified by the need to ease the administration of otherwise valid criminal laws."

California Gov. Ronald Reagan signed into law June 26, 1969 two measures restricting the sale of pornography to children. One law set up new standards of obscenity for persons under 18; the other redefined pornography and set up new fines and prison sentences. (But California voters Nov. 7, 1972 rejected a strict anti-pornography law opposed by the film industry and even some conservatives.)

The Virginia Supreme Court Sept. 5, 1969 overturned the obscenity conviction of Charles House, a Norfolk magazine distributor, and invalidated part of a state law that made possession in public of any obscene item *prima facie* evidence of a violation of the law.

The Supreme Court May 4, 1970 unanimously upheld the constitutionality of a federal statute that permitted a citizen to stop mail addressed to his home if he found it "erotically arousing or sexually provocative." The law, passed by Congress in 1967, provided that an addressee could file a notice with the Post Office declaring "in his sole discretion" that a mailing was obscene. The Post Office then had to order the sender to refrain from further mailings and delete the name of the addressee from all mailing lists owned or controlled by the sender. The statute was designed to prevent the Post Office from becoming a censor by placing the initiative for stopping offensive ads on the addressee. The court's opinion, written by Chief Justice Warren Burger, answered the argument of direct mail concerns that the law violated their rights of free speech and press. Burger, ruling in the case of *Rowan v. United States Post Office*, said communication by mail is necessary but "the right of every person 'to be let alone' must be placed in the scales with the right of others to communicate." Taking no notice of arguments that the law was being used to halt junk mail whether or not it was sexually offensive, Burger said "today's merchandising methods, the plethora of mass mailings subsidized by low postal rates, and the growth of the sale of large mailing lists . . . have changed the mailman from a carrier of primarily private communications and has made him an adjunct of the mass mailer who sends unsolicited and often unwanted mail into every home." He concluded that "Congress has erected a wall—or more accurately permits a citizen to erect a wall—that no advertiser may penetrate without his acquiescence."

The Supreme Court, in a unanimous ruling Jan. 14, 1971, declared unconstiutional two federal laws that allowed the Post Office to refuse to handle the mail of businesses selling pornographic material. A spokesman for the Post Office said, however, that the effect of the ruling was "negligible" since the laws had only been used in recent years in the two test cases before the court. The laws allowed the Post Office to impound incoming mail to a mail-order house pending a hearing determining whether the business dealt in pornographic material. In an opinion by Justice Brennan, the court said the laws violated principles laid down in a movie censorship ruling in 1965. Brennan objected that the laws placed the burden on the business to prove its material was not obscene and that there was no provision for quick judicial review of the issue. The ruling involved two mail-order businesses, the Mailbox in Los Angeles and the Book Bin in Atlanta.

The Supreme Court May 3, 1971 upheld two federal laws making it a crime to send obscene materials through the mails and forbidding the importation of pornographic material from abroad. Justice White, writing both majority opinions, conceded a "developing sentiment that adults should have complete freedom" in regard to obscenity, but he said changes in the laws should be made by the legislatures rather than the courts. In the ruling on the use of the mails, the court reversed a decision by Judge Harry Preferson of Los Angeles and reinstated an indictment against Norman G. Reidel, charged with mailing a pornographic booklet to persons who answered his advertisement in an underground newspaper. Justices Douglas and Black dissented. The second ruling, with dissents by Justices Douglas, Black and Marshall, reversed a Los Angeles federal court ruling and upheld a seizure by customs agents of obscene photographs brought from Europe by Milton Luros.

(A Gallup Poll released June 25, 1969 had reported that 85 of 100 persons interviewed favored stricter state and local laws dealing with obscenity through the mails and that 76 of every 100 wanted stricter standards applied to material sold at newsstands.)

Over the dissents of Burger and Harlan, the court June 15, 1970 reversed the obscenity conviction of Donald P. Walker, an Alliance, Ohio news dealer who had been charged with selling what a state court called "hard-core pornography." Burger wrote in his dissent, "I can find no justification, constitutional or otherwise, for this court's assuming the role of a supreme and unreviewable board of censorship for the 50 states, subjectively judging each piece of material brought before it without regard to the findings and conclusions of other courts, state or federal."

The Supreme Court ruled unanimously March 30, 1972 that the owners of drive-in movie theaters could not be punished for showing erotic movies that would not be considered obscene if shown inside unless there was a law making it clear that a more rigid standard would be applied to outdoor screens that could be seen by passing motorists and neighborhood children.

The Supreme Court ruled, 6-3, March 19, 1973 that state colleges and universities could not expel a student for distributing literature on campus they found offensive, regardless of whether it was in good taste. The University of Missouri was ordered to reinstate Barbara S. Papish, a graduate student in journalism, who was dismissed in 1969 for distributing on campus an underground newspaper that contained the words "m---f---." The majority opinion said state colleges and universities were not "enclaves immune from the sweep of the First Amendment." Justice William H. Rehnquist, joined by Burger and Blackmun in the minority opinion, argued that the majority improperly treated the case as a criminal prosecution rather than an administrative action.

(The court May 3, 1974 dismissed an appeal from a decision barring the University of Mississippi from prohibiting publication of an English department magazine "replete with four-letter words.")

The Supreme Court had ruled, 5-4, June 7, 1971 that California courts had violated the First Amendment guarantee of free speech in convicting Paul R. Cohen for disturbing the peace because he wore a jacket inscribed with a vulgarism condemning the draft. Justice Harlan called Cohen's jacket a "distasteful mode of expression," but he said the state could not make "the simple public display of this single four-letter expletive a criminal offense." Chief Justice Burger and Justices Harry A. Blackman and Black dissented. Justice White, in a partial dissent, said the case should be sent back for more evidence.

Local Standards Become the Guide

In a series of rulings the Supreme Court June 21, 1973 redefined obscenity by handing down a new set of guidelines that would enable states to ban works that were offensive to local standards. The decisions, all by 5-4 margins, reversed a 15-year court trend toward relaxation of controls against pornography. Chief Justice Burger wrote the majority opinions in each of the five cases decided. He was joined by President Nixon's appointees—Justices Harry A. Blackman, Lewis F. Powell Jr., and William H. Rehnquist—and Byron R. White.

The majority set aside the former test for obscenity—that material be "utterly without redeeming social value"—that had been established in decisions handed down by the court in 1957 and 1966. Under the new guidelines, a book, magazine, play, or motion picture would be held obscene if the "average person, applying contemporary community standards, would find that the work, taken as a whole, appeals to the prurient interest; the work depicts or describes, in a patently offensive way, sexual conduct specifically defined by applicable state law; and the work, taken as a whole, lacks serious literary, artistic, political or scientific value." Burger made it clear that a jury ruling in an obscenity case would be allowed to decide prurience on the basis of local standards, rather than a national, hypothetical definition of obscenity. "It is neither realistic nor constitutionally sound to read the First Amendment as requiring that the people of Maine or Mississippi accept public depiction of conduct found tolerable in Las Vegas or New York City."

According to the majority opinion: (a) States had to define explicitly the kinds of sexual conduct that would subject a publisher or distributor to prosecution. (b) States had the right to assume, in absence of clear proof, that there was a causal connection between pornographic material and crime and other antisocial behavior. (c) No constitutional doctrine of privacy existed that protected the display of obscene material in public places, and government limits therein did not constitute thought control. The basic case was *Miller v. California.*

The dissenting justices warned against infringement of the First Amendment, stressed the vagueness of obscenity definitions based on local community standards, and predicted citizens would be unable to determine in advance whether they would violate the law. Justice Douglas wrote: "The idea that the

First Amendment permits government to ban publications that are 'offensive' to some people puts an ominous gloss on the freedom of the press." Justice Brennan cautioned against allowing the government to decide what was moral and what was not: "For if a state may, in an effort to maintain or create a particular moral tone, prescribe what its citizens cannot read or cannot see, then it would seem to follow that in pursuit of the same objective a state could decree that its citizens must read certain books or must view certain films."

The Supreme Court affirmed by a 5-4 majority Oct. 23 the definition of obscenity it had promulgated June 21. In so doing, the court upheld one obscenity conviction, dismissed appeals on two other convictions and remanded eight other cases back to lower courts for action based on the June 21 guidelines. Dissenting in all 11 cases were Justices Douglas, Brennan, Stewart and Marshall. In a minority opinion filed in one of the cases, Douglas wrote: "Every author, every bookseller, every movie exhibitor and every librarian is now at the mercy of the local police force's conception of what appeals to prurient interest or is patently offensive. The standards can vary from town to town and day to day in an unpredictable fashion. . . . How can an author or bookseller or librarian know whether the community deems his books acceptable until after the jury renders its verdict."

Without a hearing, the Supreme Court Feb. 25, 1974 affirmed a decision declaring unconstitutional an Ohio Liquor Control Commission regulation permitting revocation of a liquor license for possession of obscene material when no judicial determination of obscenity had been made.

The court May 28, 1974 let stand a lower court ruling declaring unconstitutional a Louisiana statute requiring judges to grant injunctions against "lewd, lascivious, filthy or sexually indecent" movies or magazines at the request of a prosecutor.

The Supreme Court ruled March 18, 1975 that the City of Chattanooga, Tenn. had illegally restrained free speech by prohibiting beforehand the production of the rock musical *Hair* in a municipally-owned theater. It was the court's first decision to extend to live theater the same constitutional safeguards that already protected newspapers, books and movies against prior censorship and prohibition. By a 5-4 vote, the court held that the producers of *Hair* could be denied use of the city-owned theater prior to opening night only if Chattanooga observed certain legal procedures, including seeking a prompt court hearing, at which it would have to prove that the show was obscene. (The justices did not consider the issue of whether *Hair* was obscene.)

Writing for the majority, Justice Blackman said, "A free society prefers to punish the few who abuse rights of speech after they break the law than to throttle them and all others beforehand. It is always difficult to know in advance what an individual will say, and the line between legitimate and illegitimate speech is often so finely drawn that the risks of freewheeling censorship are formidable." Three of the dissenters—Chief Justice Burger and Justices White and Rehnquist—defended Chattanooga's right to refuse to permit the performance of *Hair*. The other dissenter, Douglas, argued that, "No matter how many procedural safeguards may be imposed, any system which permits government officials to inhibit or control the flow of disturbing and unwelcome ideas to the public threatens serious diminution of the breadth and richness of our cultural offerings."

The Supreme Court refused April 21, 1975 to review a decision reversing as unconstitutionally broad a Florida statute outlawing acts that "outrage the sense of public decency or affect the peace and quiet of persons who may witness them."

The Supreme Court June 24, 1976 upheld, 5-4 a Detroit ordinance to regulate the location of theaters showing films of explicit sexual activities or depicting "specified anatomical areas." The majority opinion, written by Justice John Paul Stevens, said that "the city's interest in attempting to preserve the quality of urban life is one that must be accorded high respect. Moreover, the city must be allowed a reasonable opportunity to experiment with solutions to admittedly serious problems." The dissenters—Justices Stewart, Blackman, Brennan and Marshall—said the majority decision would permit the right of free expression to be "defined and circumscribed by current popular opinion." The case was *Young v. American Mini Theaters.*

The Supreme Court Nov. 1, 1976 declined to review a California Supreme Court ruling that barred the city of Los Angeles from attempting to close bookstores and movie theaters on obscenity grounds. The state court had held that injunctions against particular magazines or films were permissible. It said that an attempt by the city to close a business constituted unlawful "full and pervasive prior restraint" on the freedom of expression. The case was *Van de Kamp v. Projection Room Theater.*

The Supreme Court June 6, 1977 ruled, 5-4, that the nature of advertising for allegedly pornographic material could be used by a jury in determining the verdict in an obscenity trial. The decision concerned a California man who had been convicted of selling two reels of obscene film. Prior to his conviction, the judge at his trial had told the jury to consider in its deliberation whether the film had been "commercially exploited for the sake of its prurient appeal." The defendant's attorney had argued, unsuccessfully, that advertising that was not misleading was protected by the First Amendment and could not be used to find a film obscene. In his majority opinion, Justice Rehnquist said that "evidence to pandering to prurient interests in the creation, promotion or dissemination of material is relevant in determining whether material is obscene." In a dissent joined by Justices Brennan, Stewart and Marshall, Justice Stevens contended that the ruling would permit the conviction of those whose material was not legally pornographic but which was "advertised and sold as 'sexually provocative.'" The case was *Splawn v. California.*

The Supreme Court June 9, 1977 upheld, 5-4, the 1972 obscenity conviction of a Peoria, Ill. book dealer in Illinois Supreme Court. The dealer had argued that the state's obscenity law failed to define pornography. (The law had been held unconstitutional in 1976 by a lower federal court ruling on another case.) The high court decision, in effect, restored the obscenity law.

The Supreme Court ruled unanimously March 1, 1977 that prosecutors could not seek obscenity convictions based on standards established by the high court in June 1973 if the alleged offense took place before the standards were evolved. The case, *Marks v. U.S.*, involved a distributor, Stanley Marks, who had been convicted in federal court of transporting pornographic films in interstate commerce in early 1973. The films, which included *Deep Throat*, had been shown in Newport, Ky. in February of that year, four months before the Supreme Court had handed down its tough new standards on obscenity. Marks had been found guilty under the more stringent standards. The 6th U.S. Circuit Court of Appeals had upheld his conviction.

In reversing the lower courts, the Supreme Court agreed with Marks's lawyers that he should have been prosecuted under the more liberal standards established by the high court in 1957 and 1966—rulings that had been in effect at the time of his alleged wrongdoing. The test for obscenity under those older standards required that the material in question be "utterly without redeeming social value." Justice Lewis F. Powell Jr., who wrote the opinion for the court, said that the retroactive application of the newer standards violated a defendant's due-process rights if that defendant would have been judged not guilty under the earlier, less restrictive obscenity tests.

The Supreme Court May 23, 1978 ruled, 8-1, that juries should not consider children when applying the test of "community standards" to possibly obscene material. The decision reversed the conviction of a California man for mailing pornographic advertising matter. The case was *Pinkus v. U.S.* The defendant, William Pinkus, had appealed his conviction on the ground that the judge had instructed the jury (under the court's 1973 guidelines) to consider "the community as a whole, young and old, educated and uneducated, the religious and the irreligious, men, women and children, from all walks of life." The high court, noting that there was no evidence in this case that children were the intended recipients of the material, held the judge's instruction to be improper.

Chief Justice Burger, author of the 1973 guidelines, contended in the majority opinion that jurors "conscientiously striving to define the relevant community of persons, the 'average person' by whose standards obscenity is to be judged, would reach a much lower 'average' when children are part of the equation than they would if they restricted their consideration to the effect of alleged obscene materials on adults." However, Burger maintained that juries were free to consider the possible effect of sexually explicit material on "the most susceptible or sensitive members" of the adult community, as well as the effect on "deviant sexual groups."

The Supreme Court refused to rule on another part of the Pinkus appeal: whether the commercial popularity of adult films such as *Deep Throat* should be taken into consideration by juries when applying the "community standards" test. Burger said that since the high court had reversed the conviction on another ground, it did not have to decide the question of "comparison evidence."

Justice Powell, the only dissenter, stated that the judge's instruction with regard to children was "harmless beyond a reasonable doubt."

Justice Stevens voiced disagreement with Burger's opinion, but concurred in the judgment. Justices Marshall, Stewart and Brennan voted to have the indictment dismissed.

Pornography & Crime

The Role of Organized Crime

Police and press sources assert that the pornography industry is dominated by organized crime, just as members of "the syndicate" are also said to constitute the principal controlling force in prostitution, massage parlors, topless bars, strip joints, gay bars and other enterprises on or over the borderline of respectability or illegality.

Criminal involvement in pornography was studied in 1976 by the Task Force on Organized Crime of the National Advisory Committee on Criminal Justice Standards & Goals. In its report, entitled *Organized Crime*, published in December 1976, the task force noted that "although some Mafia figures are investing in pornography, blacks, Spanish-speaking people, and other groups are now becoming more involved in the production of pornographic films."

In the Northeast, the report said, "organized crime income . . . is presently invested in a variety of business, including . . . massage parlors . . . and pornographic book stores." In this area, according to the report, "pornography . . . is showing astronomical distribution profits."

In the Southeast, the report found, "underworld organizations used all varieties of business firms," including "massage parlors as fronts for prostitution; and theaters, book stores, and film companies as fronts for pornography." Tactics used in this area include "arson—particularly in connection with pornography operations," the report said. One aspect of the situation, in the Southeast at least, is an increase in prostitution. "Prostitution is frequently linked to drug use and pornography" the report said. "The youthful performers in pornographic films are often paid in drugs for their services, then drawn into prostitution. Books, movies, and peep machines are the most common pornography enterprises; peep machines are the most lucrative. There are signs that organized crime figures from the Northeast and West are involved in pornography in this region, and that it is an extremely profitable and expansive operation. . . . Legitimate movie companies are now making X-rated movies, and there is some concern about organized crime involvement in this endeavor."

In the West, the task force found, fronts for organized crime also include "pornography enterprises. The pornography enterprises frequently entail connections between West and East coast organized crime figures, because the distribution involved in this national operation requires a network of contacts throughout the country. The major manifestations of organized crime in the West [include] . . . pornography and massage parlors. [But] law enforcement efforts and conservative community standards have served to keep these activities out of many areas."

The task force report considered the findings of the Commission on Obscenity & Pornography, which had been appointed by Lyndon B. Johnson for a 1968-70 study. The task force then reported further developments. The task force said:

"Probably the most comprehensive study of pornography was conducted by the Commission on Obscenity & Pornography from 1968 to 1970. The Commission was unable to assess the degree of involvement of organized crime, but assumed that this element might be involved because so many criminals were in the industry. The Commission did find that the pornography industry consisted of several distinct markets and submarkets, some organized, some chaotic. The wares consisted of films, magazines, books, sexual devices, and various service establishments. Subdivisions of the industry were production, distribution, and retail outlets. The market was primarily composed of white, heterosexual males. The Commission did not think that the business was overly profitable.

"Since that report, a number of studies have indicated that pornography has become organized crime's latest business. It is a logical field for entry given the facts of a prohibited product with a large market; susceptibility to good organization and muscle; and lax law enforcement.

"Just when organized crime became involved in pornography is uncertain, but a contributing factor may have been a Supreme Court decision in 1967, *Redrup v. New York*. This ruling left unclear what exactly constitutes pornography, thus making it difficult for law enforcement officers to make cases, but also making it hard for legitimate businesses to know if they were handling legal or illegal material. Thus legitimate distributors were unwilling to handle potentially pornographic material.

"That development created a situation ripe for organized crime. Al Goldstein, publisher of *Screw*, one of the better selling publications, admits freely that organized crime businesses distribute his magazine. He says that he has no choice in the matter, because no legal firms will undertake distribution. Although Goldstein has been left editorial independence, his books and production facilities are watched closely.

"Organized crime's links to the pornography industry were documented as far back as the early 1950s in the Kefauver committee investigations; but most sources show few links before the late 1960s.

"One author says that organized crime got involved in pornography in New York in 1968, when John Franzese, a member of the Colombo [crime] family, realized how profitable the peepshows in Times Square were. Subjected to typical strongarm tactics, the owners soon had to give organized crime 50 percent of their profits. From there, it was but a short step to insisting that all outlets use projection machines supplied by organized crime. By 1969, the Colombo family had obtained about 60 percent control of the porno movies in New York.

"Organized crime is believed to be in all aspects of the pornography industry: literature and films of all types (i.e., hard core, soft core, art, 16mm, magazines, books), sexual devices, 'service' establishments (including live sex shows), production, wholesaling and retailing, and distribution.

"For example, Michael Zaffarano of the Bonano family is said to be a major operator on both the east and west coasts. He is involved in the production and distribution of films and owns theaters. He also finances production of films through many legitimate fronts.

"The Peraino brothers, informally adopted members of the Colombo family, are said to be the biggest in the business. They, too, operate behind various legal fronts headquartered in New Jersey and Florida. They are said to have put up the money for 'Deep Throat,' one of the most successful of pornographic films, which has grossed at least $25 million. With the proceeds of that venture, the Perainos set up Bryanston Distributors, which is involved in legitimate films such as Andy Warhol's 'Frankenstein.' In fact, one New York City police official fears that organized crime eventually could become a major factor in the legitimate film industry.

"Organized crime also has become heavily involved in the distribution of pornographic materials. The two distributors of *Screw* were once legitimate companies that suddenly developed very strong organized crime ties about the time that recent Supreme Court decisions scared off legal distributors. Star Distributors in Manhattan is one of the largest national distributors (its position is enhanced by its exclusive rights to *Screw*), while Astro News of Brooklyn handles the New York City market.

"Some independent producers say they actually prefer dealing with organized crime enterprises because the latter are the most reliable of companies and pay quickly. Others find that they must deal with organized crime in order to protect themselves from extortion or piracy.

"Piracy is a big part of organized crime's pornography business. If a producer refuses to allow organized crime figures to distribute a film, those figures threaten piracy, among other actions. If its request is still refused, organized crime elements make their own copies of the film and distribute them widely, very often closing substantial markets to the legitimate producer.

"The fate of 'Behind the Green Door,' another successful porn movie, is a case in point. Organized crime figures approached the producers concerning distribution rights, which the producers continuously refused to grant, despite threats of piracy. Within a short time, hundreds of pirate versions appeared all over the country. The producers lost several key markets—Las Vegas, Miami, and Dallas among them. Also, because the pirated versions were often of poor quality, the movie got a bad reputation, which further reduced its market.

"According to one source, few independents in any area of the industry can escape the influence of organized crime. Says this observer: 'Combining old-fashioned muscle with sizeable payoffs to cops and politicians, Mafia dons from coast to coast make sure no dirty magazine, hard-core film or peep show machine enters their city without the payment of tribute to the local crime family.'

"The centers of organized crime's pornography activities are Los Angeles and New York City. The New York police estimate that three out of five Italian crime families are involved in the New York business and are responsible for 90 percent of the pornography in the area.

"Organized crime's operations actually blanket the country. A former Dallas chief of police said: 'The pornography business in Dallas has all the earmarks of an organized crime operation. We have learned that the organizations in Dallas are linked to an organization which owns and controls the production, printing, distribution, and retail sale outlets for pornographic material.'

"No accurate figures exist on what profits organized crime receives from the industry, but money must be good or organized crime would not be involved. One source puts the gross from peepshows in Baltimore alone at about $10 million a year in 1973, while another says that each peepshow machine earns $10,000 a year. A third source says that a high quality, 12-minute pornographic film takes about an hour to make at a cost of $3 (the actors and actresses are paid in drugs), and sells for about $50.

"Prosecution of organized crime pornography operations has been very difficult. In New York City, for example, this legal action has run up against not only the Supreme Court's imprecise definition of pornography, but also the slowness of the court system and the lack of city resources. If a film is declared pornographic, the producer simply doctors it enough to qualify it as a new film, forcing the city to go through a long, expensive court procedure all over again. In the meantime, the film is shown.

"Licensing and code violation enforcement has also had little success against pornography, because most violations are eventually corrected. Also, organized crime lawyers file a steady stream of challenges to new laws or regulations, especially zoning laws, and have even sued a city for harassment. All this means more delay and expense for the city and continued operations for organized crime. Some cities have more or less compromised. Boston, for example, has opted for a policy of containment to a certain part of town—the so-called Washington Street 'combat zone.' "

The extensive influence of organized crime in American business, politics and society had emerged as a subject of local and national concern in 1977. Attention focused on the underworld's infiltration of previously legitimate industries and its migration to Southern and Western states. The Federal Bureau of Investigation estimated that the 26 Mafia (*Cosa Nostra*) families had a total membership of about 5,000. It was estimated that the Mafia took in at least $48 billion annually in gross revenues and netted $25 billion in untaxed profits. Besides continuing to dominate gambling, loan sharking, prostitution and labor racketeering, the Justice Department said, the Mafia might own as many as 10,000 legitimate firms, such as banks, hotels, restaurants and construction companies. The expanded influence of organized crime was particularly strong in the expensive "Sunbelt" retirement colonies of Florida, California and Arizona. The June 13 issue of *U.S. News and World Report* noted a marked influx of underworld figures into those states during the early 1970s because of pressure from law enforcement officials in New Jersey. The Federal Task Force on Organized Crime reported that Fort Lauderdale, Fla. "seems to be the center for financial fraud for the entire nation."

The *Miami Herald* reported June 19 that in Florida, as elsewhere, organized crime almost completely controlled the distribution of pornographic books, magazines and films. The mob, alert to the nation's change in moral attitudes and sexual permissiveness, saw the opportunity to exploit a new illicit activity with high profit potential. The *St. Louis Post-Dispatch* reported July 3 that an Atlanta-based nationwide Mafia syndicate was controlling the pornography racket in St. Louis and that the same group served more than 100 dealers in the western U.S. According to the Atlanta Police Department's intelligence division, the same organized crime figures were involved in pornography in Los Angeles, Atlanta, Chicago and South Florida. The Atlanta police also linked Atlanta's pornography operation to New York Mafia chieftain Carmine Galante and to Frank Bompensiero, a leading San Diego crime figure who was slain Feb. 10, apparently to prevent him from testifying before a federal grand jury probing Mafia ties to the pornography industry. Bompensiero, 71, a *consigliere* (third-ranking member) in the Mafia, also had been the FBI's highest-placed informer. He was one of some 20 mysterious murder victims since December 1973, many of whom had been expected to testify against underworld figures.

Thevis One of 'Ten Most Wanted Fugitives'

Michael George Thevis, described as a multimillionaire pornographer with nationwide organized crime connections, was added July 10, 1978 to the FBI's list of "Ten Most Wanted Fugitives."

Thevis, already serving a federal sentence for interstate transportation in aid of racketeering-arson and interstate transportation of obscene matter, was awaiting transfer when he escaped from the Floyd County Jail, New Albany, Ind., in April 1978 by walking out of a side door, the Department of Justice said.

Thevis' arrest record dated back to 1949. His arrests were mostly on charges of transportation of obscene matter. He reportedly had built a web of some 238 corporations through which he controlled 40 percent of the country's pornography business. His real estate and property holdings, including an Atlanta home with over 30,000 square feet of space, was said to be worth over $100 million.

In May 1978, Thevis was indicted by a federal grand jury in Indianapolis on charges of prison escape. One month later, he was indicted by a federal grand jury in Atlanta on charges of violating the Racketeer Influenced & Corrupt Organizations Statute by crimes that allegedly included two murders, three acts of arson, four acts involving obstruction of justice for allegedly attempting to kill a government witness, one count of extortion and one count of mail fraud. Most of the charges against Thevis stem from his alleged attempts to thwart business competition or government investigation of his activities.

Is Pornography a Cause of Sex Crime?

Several studies have attempted to determine whether exposure to pornography was a cause of sex crime. The studies appeared to be generally inconclusive. In some cases it appeared that persons convicted of such crimes had a greater degree of exposure to pornography than the average. The possibility was suggested, however, that people who commit sex crimes were more attracted to pornography—or less inhibited in chosing to use it—than non-criminals but that the exposure to pornography was not necessarily involved in their criminal acts and in some cases may have followed them.

In its 1970 report, the Commission on Obscenity & Pornography cited a study in which M. Lipkin and D. E. Carns sought to

ESCAPED FEDERAL PRISONER; RACKETEER INFLUENCED AND CORRUPT
ORGANIZATIONS - MURDER, ARSON; MAIL FRAUD; CONSPIRACY

WANTED BY FBI

MICHAEL GEORGE THEVIS

Entered NCIC
I. O. 4805
6-28-78

FBI No. 672,805 C

NCIC: 15TT07XX080154TT1208

15 M 1 T 8 AMP Ref: U/R

S 1 Rt

ALIASES: George Thevis, M. G. Thevis, Michael Thevis, Michael G. Thevis, Micheal George Thevis, Mike Thevis

Photograph taken 1970

Photographs taken 1974

DESCRIPTION

AGE: 46, born February 25, 1932, Raleigh, North Carolina (not supported by birth records)
HEIGHT: 5'10"
WEIGHT: 170 to 175 pounds
BUILD: medium
HAIR: brown - balding
EYES: brown
COMPLEXION: medium
RACE: white
NATIONALITY: American
OCCUPATIONS: corporation president, newsstand operator, publisher, restaurant operator
SCARS AND MARKS: scars on right temple, left side of nose, under chin and both legs; first two joints of right ring finger amputated
REMARKS: may walk with limp, wear brace on left leg and use cane due to hip disorder; may be clean shaven; known to spend excessively
SOCIAL SECURITY NUMBER USED: 266-40-2390

CRIMINAL RECORD

Thevis has been convicted of interstate transportation of obscene matter and conspiracy to commit arson.

CAUTION

THEVIS, A NATIONALLY KNOWN DISTRIBUTOR OF PORNOGRAPHY, IS BEING SOUGHT AS AN ESCAPEE FROM CUSTODY AND FOR HIS ALLEGED PARTICIPATION IN TWO MURDERS AND FOUR ATTEMPTS TO KILL GOVERNMENT WITNESSES. BECAUSE THEVIS HAS USED FIREARMS AND EXPLOSIVE DEVICES IN THE PAST, HE SHOULD BE CONSIDERED ARMED, DANGEROUS, AND AN ESCAPE RISK.

A Federal warrant was issued on May 17, 1978, at Indianapolis, Indiana, charging Thevis with violation of the Escape and Rescue Statute (Title 18, U. S. Code, Section 751(a)). A Federal warrant was also issued on June 12, 1978, at Atlanta, Georgia, charging Thevis with violation of the Racketeer Influenced and Corrupt Organizations Statute (Title 18, U. S. Code, Sections 1961, 1962(c), and 1963); mail fraud, conspiracy, obstruction of criminal investigation, and obstruction of justice (Title 18, U. S. Code, Sections 1341, 371, 1510, and 1503), respectively.

IF YOU HAVE INFORMATION CONCERNING THIS PERSON, PLEASE CONTACT YOUR LOCAL FBI OFFICE. TELEPHONE NUMBERS AND ADDRESSES OF ALL FBI OFFICES LISTED ON BACK.

Identification Order 4805
June 28, 1978

Director
Federal Bureau of Investigation
Washington, D. C. 20535

determine whether exposure to pornography was a factor in causing antisocial behavior. They received answers from 35 percent of the 7,484 psychiatrists and 3,078 clinical psychologists to whom they sent queries. The questions and answers follow:

"In your professional experience, have you encountered any cases where it appeared that pornography was a causal factor in antisocial behavior?"

| Yes, convinced | 7.4% | No such cases | 80 |
| Yes, suspected | 9.4 | Not ascertained | 3.2 |

"Persons exposed to pornography are more likely to engage in antisocial acts than persons not exposed."

| Strongly agree | 1.1 | Disagree | 56.4 |
| Agree | 12.9 | Strongly disagree | 27.3 |

The experience of Denmark was said by some to indicate that the availability of pornography did not result in an increase in sex crime and may even cause a decline in such behavior. Laws against printed pornography had been repealed in Denmark as of July 1967, and two years later Denmark had similarly ended laws against pictorial pornography for anybody above the age of 16. The U.S. Commission on Obscenity & Pornography noted that between 1965 and 1970, the number of sex offenses reported against women in Copenhagen had declined from 723 to 310, the cases of exhibitionism from 203 to 84, instances reported of peeping from 76 to 11 and of child-molestation from more than 200 to 100. But former U.S. Postmaster General Winton M. Blount charged in the September 1971 issue of *Nation's Business* "that this is largely a statistical trick. Pornography used to be a crime there and now it isn't. Therefore the crime rate has dropped. Statutory rape used to be a crime there; now it isn't. . . . Minor crimes, such as indecent exposure, are scarcely even reported. The 'crime rate' argument is a misleading and foolish bit of whimsy. Postal officials have gone to Denmark and talked to the authorities there and found that the real sex crime rate has not dropped."

Dealing with Pornography

The volume of pornography consumed by Americans increased tremendously during the 1960s and on past the mid-1970s despite government and other efforts to control it. A number of significant developments involving this issue are related below. These accounts are largely based on the record compiled by FACTS ON FILE in its weekly coverage of current world history.

Pornography Commission's Report

An 18-member Commission on Obscenity & Pornography had been appointed by former President Lyndon B. Johnson Jan. 2, 1968 to study the relationship between pornography and antisocial behavior, particularly in minors. After a two-year study, the commission issued its report in September 1970. But even before the report was issued it came under attack, by President Richard M. Nixon among others, for opposing bans on pornography for adults and for finding that pornography apparently was not a significant cause of antisocial behavior.

Pornography report disclaimed. The Nixon Administration rejected the rec-

ommendations of the President's Commission on Obscenity and Pornography Aug. 11, 1970 even though the group's report had not been approved by the panel or released.

At a White House news briefing, Press Secretary Ronald L. Ziegler said while "There is no intent to prejudge the findings of the report," President Nixon had feelings at variance with the commission's recommendations, included in a draft of the report leaked earlier to a House subcommittee.

Ziegler, who commented on the subject without being asked, said: "This is not Nixon's commission. It was formed under a previous administration. He did not appoint the members and the commission's recommendations are not those of this administration."

A House Post Office and Civil Service subcommittee held hearings on the

draft report Aug. 11–12. After Ziegler's press conference, Rep. Robert N.C.
Nix (D, Pa.), the subcommittee chairman, released letters to President Nixon
written by his only appointee to the
commission, Charles H. Keating Jr., a
founder of Citizens for Decent Literature Inc. Keating warned Nixon that
the commission planned to recommend
the repeal of all U.S. laws against pornography for adults.

The 18-member commission said in
its draft report "there is no evidence
that exposure to pornography operates
as a cause of misconduct in either youths
or adults" and said research indicated
that "erotic materials do not contribute
to the development of character deficits,
nor operate as a significant factor in
antisocial behavior or in crime and delinquency causation."

Report released & attacked. After long
controversy, the report of the President's
Commission on Obscenity & Pornography
was released Sept. 30, 1970 amid
continued criticism of the entire report
and its most controversial recommendation—the repeal of all legislation prohibiting sale of sexual material to consenting adults. The 622-page majority
report, prepared after two years of research at a cost of nearly $2 million,
drew strong attacks from dissenting
members of the commission, from con-
gressmen and from the Nixon Administration.

In presenting the report, William B.
Lockhart, dean of the University of Minnesota Law School and chairman of the
commission, defended the panel's efforts
against attacks by a leading dissenter,
Charles H. Keating Jr.

Keating charged that Lockhart and
other commissioners held "highly slanted
and biased" preconceptions and that the
commission staff, directed by Dr. W. Cody
Wilson, had led the research toward pre-
determined conclusions. Keating contended that repeal of pornography legislation in Denmark had led to "animalism
and paganism."

Keating's position was supported by
two commission members—the Rev.
Morton A. Hill, president of Morality

and Media, a New York organization;
and the Rev. Winfrey C. Link, a Methodist minister of Nashville, Tenn. In a dissent, Link and Hill condemned the majority report as a "magna carta for the
pornographer." Attorney General
Thomas C. Lynch of California also dissented.

Two commissioners—Rabbi Irving
Lehrman of Miami Beach and Mrs.
Cathryn A. Spelts of the South Dakota
School of Mines—supported the bulk of
the report but said there was insufficient
evidence available to warrant repeal of
pornography laws for adults.

In recommending repeal of laws concerning consenting adults, the 12-man
majority said it found "no evidence that
exposure to or use of explicit sexual
materials play a significant role in the
causation of social or individual harms
such as crime, delinquency, sexual or
nonsexual deviancy or severe emotional
disturbances." The majority did advocate
legislation to prohibit sale of "certain
sexual materials to young persons" and
laws agains "public displays of sexually
explicit pictorial materials."

Two commissioners—Otto N. Larsen,
professor of sociology at the University
of Washington, and Marvin E. Wolf-
gang, director of the University of Pennsylvania's Center of Criminological
Research—said all pornography laws
should be repealed because such legislation was "ambiguous, often unenforce-
able." They said "informal social controls will work better without the confusion of ambiguous and arbitrarily administered laws."

The majority gave perhaps the greatest emphasis to its recommendation that
a "massive" sex education effort be
launched to "contribute to healthy attitudes" toward sex and to "provide a
sound foundation for our society's basic
institution of marriage and family." The
majority recommended that sex education in the U.S. "allow for a pluralism of
values" and include training for parents,
teachers, doctors, clergy and social workers. The panel also urged continued open
discussion and research on pornography.

Other members of the commission—
all supporting the majority position—
were Frederick H. Wagman, director of

the University of Michigan library (vice chairman); Edward E. Elson, president of the Atlanta News Agency; Chief Judge Thomas D. Gill of the Hartford, Conn., Juvenile Court; Edward D. Greenwood, psychiatrist at the Menninger Clinic in Topeka, Kan.; G. William Jones, Southern Methodist University (Dallas) assistant professor of broadcast film art; Joseph T. Klapper, Columbia Broadcasting System's director of social research; Freedman Lewis, retired vice president of Pocket Books, New York; Morris A. Lipton, University of North Carolina professor of psychiatry; and Barbara Scott, deputy attorney of the Motion Picture Association of America.

Reaction—Hours after the report was released, Vice President Spiro T. Agnew attacked its conclusions and said, "As long as Richard Nixon is President, Main Street is not going to turn into Smut Alley." Campaigning in Salt Lake City, Agnew also charged that an "increasing depravity has been encouraged by court decision" in pornography cases.

Among other Administration spokesmen who denounced the report were Postmaster General Winton M. Blount—in speeches before the Chamber of Commerce in Nashville Sept. 28 and Kansas City, Mo. Oct. 1—and Presidential counselor Robert H. Finch in an Oct. 2 statement released by the White House. Finch, who said he spoke "as a parent and private citizen and as an official of the federal government," denounced the majority recommendations as "counsels of irresponsibility."

Senate Democratic leader Mike Mansfield of Montana said Oct. 1 that he disagreed that pornography did no harm to adults and added, "I think we've been pretty free with our permissiveness in this area." Senate minority whip Robert P. Griffin of Michigan Oct. 1 urged a "tightening of control rather than moving in the direction of the commission."

Nixon repudiates pornography report. President Nixon, in a statement released in Baltimore Oct. 24, criticized what he called the "morally bankrupt conclusions" of the President's Commission on Obscenity and Pornography. Pointing out that the commission had been appointed by a previous administration, he said he "totally" rejected the report.

The President, whose comments were released during a campaign appearance on behalf of Maryland GOP candidates, said: "So long as I am in the White House, there will be no relaxation of the national effort to control and eliminate smut from our national life." He said pornography "should be outlawed in every state in the union" and called on federal and state legislatures and courts to "act in unison to achieve that goal."

Nixon said the "warped and brutal portrayal of sex, ... if not halted and reversed, could poison the well-springs of American and Western culture and civilization." He said "American morality is not to be trifled with" and that the commission "has performed a disservice."

William B. Lockhart, chairman of the commission, said Oct. 25 that the President had attacked the report because the panel's "scientific studies do not support the assumptions congenial to his viewpoint." He said he hoped that after the November elections, the commission's findings would be reviewed "in a calm atmosphere uncharged with election appeals."

The Senate denounced the pornography report in a resolution passed by a 60-5 roll-call vote Oct. 13. Sen. John L. McClellan (D, Ark.), chief sponsor of the resolution, charged that the commission was "slanted and biased in favor of protecting the business of obscenity and pornography which the commission was mandated by Congress to regulate."

The President had been urged by 33 Republican senators Oct. 10 to reject the commission's report, particularly its recommendation to repeal pornography laws pertaining to adults.

Crime commission rejects pornography toleration. Among proposals covering most aspects of federal criminal law, the National Commission on Reform of Federal Criminal Laws—in a Jan. 7, 1971 draft of a new code—urged that laws against the sale and distribution of pornography be retained. The panel said it had considered and rejected recommendations by the President's Commission on Obscenity and Pornography that pornography laws concerning adults be abolished.

The panel urged that homosexuality and other deviate sexual activity among consenting adults not be considered criminal.

Nixon bill attacks obscenity. The Nixon Administration submitted to Congress March 22, 1973 legislation calling for the first complete revision of the U.S. criminal codes since 1790.

The Nixon bill also provided for the toughening of the definition of obscenity. Obscene material would be defined as explicit detailing of sexual intercourse, violence involving sado-masochistic sex, or an explicit, close-up view of human genitalia. Such material would be banned if it constituted a major portion of a work, if it was not necessary to maintain the integrity of the work, and if it pandered primarily to prurient interests. Conviction under the proposed statute called for up to three years in jail.

Motion Pictures

New codes tried. Two new codes were adopted by the motion picture industry in the 1960s in at least partial response to pressure against an alleged growth of obscenity in films and other complaints.

The board of directors of the Motion Picture Association of America (MPAA) Sept. 20, 1966 unanimously adopted a new Production Code to regulate the contents and treatment of films produced by major U.S. film companies. This was the first major revision of the code since its adoption in 1930. The new code, besides eliminating many specific taboos (the old code had contained prohibitions against "lustful kissing" and passion that "stimulates the baser emotions"), gave the code office authority to designate certain approved

films as "recommended for mature audiences."

MPAA President Jack J. Valenti said the new code had two principal objectives: (1) "To encourage artistic expression by expanding creative freedom, and (2) to assure that the freedom that encourages the artists remains responsible and sensitive to the standards of the larger society." The code also provided for the establishment of a Motion Picture Code Board to hear appeals from producers whose films were denied the code seal or from producers who felt their films did not require a "mature audiences" rating.

Under the new code:

(a) "Restraint shall be exercised in portraying the taking of life."

(b) "Evil, sin, crime and wrongdoing shall not be justified."

(c) "Special restraint shall be exercised in portraying criminal or antisocial activities in which minors participate or are involved."

(d) "Detailed and protracted acts of brutality, cruelty, physical violence, torture and abuse shall not be presented."

(e) "Indecent or undue exposure of the human body shall not be presented."

(f) "Illicit sex relationships shall not be justified. Intimate sex scenes violating common standards of decency shall not be portrayed. Restraint and care shall be exercised in presentations dealing with sex aberrations."

(g) "Obscene speech, gestures or movements shall not be presented. Undue profanity should not be permitted."

(h) "Religion shall not be demeaned."

(i) "Words or symbols contemptuous of racial, religious or national groups, shall not be used so as to incite hatred."

(j) "Excessive cruelty to animals shall not be portrayed, and animals shall not be treated inhumanely."

The new code, however, proved ineffective, and representatives of major U.S. film producers and exhibitors announced Oct. 7, 1968 that they had agreed on a new classification code for films. There had been growing public concern over increased violence and sex in films, and the industry had been threatened with government intervention.

Valenti asserted that the new rating system, which classified U.S.-made films into four categories, was designed both to give film makers greater freedom of expression and to safeguard children from the possible ill effects of the new freedoms. Starting Nov. 1, each picture was to be rated independently on a voluntary basis by the Production Code Administration, a branch of the MPAA, headed by Geoffrey Shurlock.

The classification categories:

G—suggested for general audiences
M—for adults and mature young people
R—restricted to those 16 or older, unless the younger patrons were accompanied by a parent or guardian
X—those under 16 not admitted.

Reaction to the code was generally favorable. The National Catholic Office for Motion Pictures and the Broadcasting & Film Commission of the National Council of Churches, in a joint statement issued Oct. 8, gave the plan their "full and genuine support." The Rev. Patrick J. Sullivan, director of the Catholic group (formerly known as the National Legion of Decency), said that if the code were implemented conscientiously, it would eliminate the need for the office to classify films.

Walter Reade Jr., president of the Walter Reade Organization, a major film exhibition and distribution company, was the first major film executive to voice opposition to the code. In an address to the National Theater Owners of America in San Francisco Nov. 10, Reade attacked the plan as a form of censorship that was both impractical and undesireable. The code's primary weakness, he said, was that it could be implemented only on a voluntary basis.

Valenti Jan. 27, 1970 announced major changes in the MPAA's already revised film classification system. The "M" category ("for adults and mature young people") was redesignated "GP," or "general patronage," with all ages admitted but parental guidance suggested. The suggested age limit for the categories "R" (barred to unaccompanied young people) and "X" (barred to all young people) was raised from 16 to 17.

The changes were decided on after an MPAA-commissioned survey had revealed public confusion over the meaning of the ratings; the changes were adopted partly as a result of public concern over

the possible effects on young people of recent graphic, sexually oriented films. To handle disputes over particular rating decisions, an advisory group of film critics and teachers was to be formed.

A breakdown by categories of films rated in 1969 was made public Jan. 28. Of 364 films, 101 (27.7%) were rated "G" (all ages admitted); 150 (41%) received the old "M" rating; 90 (25%) were rated "R"; and 23 (6.3%) were rated "X."

Valenti, testifying Jan. 28 before a House Judiciary subcommittee hearing on anti-obscenity legislation, said that the industry's voluntary rating system eliminated the need for federal legislation.

A little over a year later *The New York Times* reported (April 19, 1971) that of 1,117 films submitted for classification since the rating code went into effect, 283 were rated "G," 416 were rated "GP," 335 were rated "R" and 83 were rated "X."

The number of X-rated films being shown numbered "perhaps 300," according to a member of the association's rating administration, since many producers applied their own X rating. The trend among major film producers, however, was away from detailed exploration of sex. Several companies were reported to have banned all X-rated films. Among the reasons for the shift were notable successes by films catering to all levels, complaints against X-rated films and "a remarkable reversal in taste" in the whole country, according to Metro-Goldwyn-Mayer President James Aubrey.

Church groups reject industry ratings—Citing the unreliability of the GP rating, the Protestant and Catholic motion picture review panels withdrew their support of the film industry's ratings system, the New York Times reported May 19, 1971. The Broadcasting & Film Commission of the National Council of Churches and the National Catholic Office for Motion Pictures said the GP rating had been given to several films that merited the R designation because of the nature of their subject matter.

The Rev. Patrick J. Sullivan, director of the Catholic group, explained that the industry's rating system over-emphasized overt visual sex and gave little consideration to "the implicit exploitation of sex and the overall impact of violence and other antisocial aspects of the film . . ." Among the films whose GP ratings were questioned were 10 *Rillington Place, Valdez Is Coming, Bananas* and *That Splendid November.*

Jack Valenti, president of the Motion Picture Association of America, charged May 19 that the religious groups' actions were a "possibly unconscious attempt" to bring about government censorship by destroying public confidence in the ratings system. Spokesmen for the religious groups denied the charges.

While admitting the system was "flawed," Valenti said a "scientific survey" conducted for his office by the Opinion Research Corp. of Princeton showed that 64% of 2,600 persons surveyed said the ratings were useful in selecting films for their children.

Action vs. 'obscenity' in 1969. Facing increased pressure to curb violence, nudity and "obscenity" in the arts, the federal government and various other organizations made several attempts during 1969 to censor offensive material.

The trend as far as motion pictures was concerned was toward more candid treatment of lovemaking, including that of homosexuals, and veered away from the extreme violence and sadism of earlier Western and gangster movies. Although very few films were actually barred to the public, about 30% of those released since November 1968 (when the new (1966) rating system went into effect had been given "R" or "X" ratings, Jack Valenti, president of the Motion Picture Association of America, reported Oct. 10, 1979.

The most controversial film released during 1969 was the Swedish import *I Am Curious (Yellow),* the first of a two-part feature dealing with contemporary Swedish life, which showed several explicit sex scenes. It opened in New York March 10 after the U.S. Court of Appeals ruled it

was not obscene. By Sept. 29 the film had grossed $5,151,486 in the U.S. The film was judged obscene by Chief Justice G. Joseph Tauro of the Suffolk Superior Court in Boston Nov. 12. He fined its distributor, Film Distributors, Inc., $5,000, Seraphim Karalekis, manager of the Symphony Cinema (where the film was shown), $500 and sentenced the theater's president, James Vlamos, to a one-year prison term. DeVisser Theaters, Inc. of Closter, N.J. Nov. 25 agreed not to show the film in any of its Passaic County (N.J.) theaters after a suit was brought against the concern by Passaic County Prosecutor John G. Thevos. Superior Court Judge Paul W. La Prade Dec. 8 found the film obscene and barred its showing in Arizona.

According to Edward de Grazia, a Washington lawyer who represented Grove Press, the nationwide distributor of *I Am Curious (Yellow),* legal actions to bar the movie had been largely unsuccessful. De Grazia said Nov. 24 that the film had been contested in only 15 of the 53 cities in which it had been released and said it had been closed down in only three—Kansas City, Boston and Baltimore.

Over the dissent of Justice William O. Douglas, the Supreme Court Dec. 15 set aside a federal court injunction against further prosecution for showing *I Am Curious (Yellow)* in Boston. Distributors of the Swedish film had obtained the injunction after an obscenity conviction for showing the film. Douglas said he always dissented from rulings that upheld censorship "but not because, as frequently charged, I relish 'obscenity.' " (The court March 23 had reversed, 6–2, a Kentucky state court's ruling that the film *I, a Woman* was obscene. The case: *Cain v. Kentucky.*)

Connecticut motion picture theater managers March 26 complied with an order to delete a five-minute scene of lovemaking between two lesbians from *The Killing of Sister George.* The scene reportedly violated the state's obscenity and licensing law. (Under a similar Massachusetts law, a Boston theater manager was fined $1,000 and sentenced to six months in prison in March because he showed the film in its unabridged form.)

Alabama state police, acting under orders from Gov. Albert P. Brewer, July 9 seized six films being shown at drive-in theaters throughout Alabama and charged the theater managers with violation of a 1907 anti-obscenity law that prohibited any display of nudity except in art galleries. The films seized were *Inga, Starlet, Thar She Blows, Barbette, The Shanty Tramp* and *The Secret Lives of Romeo and Juliet.*

Artist Andy Warhol's *Blue Movie,* released in New York July 21, was declared hard-core pornography (and therefore in violation of New York's penal code) by a three-judge panel in Criminal Court Sept. 17.

The Texas State Senate voted 21–9 Sept. 3 to impose a "dirty movie" tax of $1 on all films bearing an "X" rating as well as on all unrated movies produced prior to November 1968 which did not bear the "Code Seal of Approval" of the Motion Picture Association of America.

U.S. Customs Oct. 2 seized the Swedish import *Language of Love* on grounds that it was obscene and immoral. Imported by Unicorn Enterprises of New York, the film illustrated sexual anxieties and responses in a medical background.

(The Italian Association of Cinema Authors June 20 expelled Franco Zeffirelli, director of *Romeo and Juliet,* because of his opposition to the new trend of erotic films. The group said "any pornography or morbidity is preferable to [the] repression" Zeffirelli sought.)

Maryland ban on 'Curious' upheld— The Supreme Court, deadlocked March 8, 1971 over the question of whether *I Am Curious (Yellow)* was obscene, upheld the right of the Maryland Board of Censors to ban it. The 4–4 ruling in effect affirmed lower court ruling in favor of the ban, but the decision would have no weight as a precedent.

Justice Douglas abstained from the case, as he had done in other cases involving Grove Press, which had published an excerpt from one of his books in its *Evergreen Review.* Pointing out that Justice Douglas in virtually all cases held against censorship in any form, a lawyer for Grove Press said the decision meant that "anyone but Grove Press can dis-tribute a movie like this" since Douglas would be free to participate in other obscenity cases.

'Deep Throat' rejected by judge. New York Criminal Court Judge Joel L. Tyler ruled in New York City March 1, 1973 that the film *Deep Throat* was "indisuptably and irredeemably" obscene. In his opinion, Tyler called the film a "feast of carrion and squalor," "a nadir of decadence" and "brazenly explicit." "This is one throat that deserves to be cut," Tyler wrote.

New York City had brought charges of promoting obscenity against the theater showing *Deep Throat* Aug. 17 and 29, 1972. Tyler began hearing the case without a jury, Dec. 18, 1972, as prescribed in New York laws charging corporations with misdemeanors.

Mature Enterprises, Inc., principal exhibitor of the film, was fined $100,000 by Judge Tyler April 12.

Deep Throat was estimated to have grossed more than $1 million in New York City and $4 million more across the nation, *The New York Times* reported March 2. It was distributed nationwide by Sherpix, Inc.

Ohio ban rejected. The Supreme Court Nov. 12, 1973 rejected a state ban on allegedly obscene motion pictures.

The court upheld a lower court ruling barring Ohio authorities from forbidding the showing of films they deemed obscene, which had not been ruled obscene through prior adversary hearings.

Court narrows 1973 ruling's scope. The Supreme Court ruled June 24, 1974 that the film *Carnal Knowledge* was not obscene under guidelines promulgated by the count in 1973.

Carnal Knowledge, a film that depicted the contrasting sex lives and marriages of two friends from their college years to middle age, was declared obscene by an Albany, Ga. jury. The Georgia Supreme Court, applying the high court's 1973 obscenity standards, upheld the Albany jury.

"Our own view of the film," Justice William Rehnquist wrote for the unanimous court, "satisfies us that [it] . . . could not be found under the [court's 1973] standards to depict sexual conduct in a patently offensive way." It was a "serious misreading" of the 1973 decision to conclude that juries had "unbridled discretion" to decide what was obscene, Rehnquist said. The 1973 guidelines were established to proscribe hard-core pornography, not whatever a jury found distasteful, he stated.

In a concurring opinion, Justices Brennan, Stewart and Marshall argued that the obscenity case helped bear out their predictions that the court would become "mired" in a case-by-case review of each questionable book, movie and magazine. The only way out, they said, was to outlaw all suppression except where juveniles were concerned. In another concurring opinion, Justice Douglas maintained his opposition to any kind of censorship.

Drive-in curb rejected. The Supreme Court June 23, 1975 invalidated a local ordinance curbing films at drive-in theaters.

The court struck down as an unconstitutional interference with free speech a Jacksonville, Fla. ordinance making drive-in theaters and their employes criminally liable for showing films containing nudity that were visible outside the theater grounds. "The Constitution does not permit the government to decide which types of otherwise protected speech are sufficiently offensive to require protection for unwilling viewers or listeners" on public streets, the court said. Chief Justice Warren Burger and Justices Byron White and William Rehnquist dissented.

Live Theater

Sex & nudity under attack. A drive toward censorship in the theater got under way in 1969. It was aimed primarily at increased nudity, which had come to Broadway April 29, 1968 with the rock musical *Hair,* and at the "explicit" portrayal of sexual relations. Among the developments of 1969:

The first play to depict sexual relations on stage was *Che,* which opened in New York March 22. A one-act drama written by Lennox Raphael, 29, it portrayed symbolically the last hours of Cuban guerrilla leader Ernesto Che Guevara. The cast and production staff were arrested March 24 and charged with consensual sodomy, public lewdness and obscenity.

Oh! Calcutta!, an off-Broadway revue performed almost completely in the nude, opened in New York June 17. Devised by British theater manager Kenneth Tynan, who described the show as "an elegant evening of erotica," the play included material written by Samuel Beckett, Jules Feiffer, Tennessee Williams, John Lennon and Bruce Jay Friedman. Seven cast members and the producer of the Los Angeles *Calcutta* troupe were arrested Dec. 17 and charged with lewd conduct and indecent exposure.

Ten cast members who had appeared nude in a production of *Dionysus in 69* at the University of Michigan were arrested Jan. 26.

Actors Equity Association announced rules May 19 for performers required to appear nude in New York shows. The union declared that its members must be given prior notice if their roles called for "nudity and/or simulated sex acts" and that no performer could be required to disrobe until he had been auditioned as an actor, singer or dancer.

Broadcasting

FCC to probe obscenity. The Federal Communications Commission (FCC) said March 27, 1973 that it had voted, 5-1, March 22 to investigate alleged obscenity on radio and TV stations for possible law violations.

The FCC had received 3,000 complaints since December 1972 about alleged obscenity, mostly concerning late night radio call-in shows, during which some women allegedly discussed their sex life in graphic detail, a few cases of pornographic movie showings on cable or commercial stations and obscene language and displays of sexual organs on public access programs in two major cities.

The commission had been questioned about the complaints during Congressional hearings by Sen. John O. Pastore (D, R.I.), and by Rep. Torbert H. MacDonald (D, Mass.) March 14. MacDonald said March 27 he was "delighted that [FCC Chairman Dean] Burch and a majority of his fellow commissioners have acted with such dispatch."

Nicholas Johnson, the only commissioner to dissent, said the "FCC has no business listening to subject matter of programs," except in determining the percentage of program categories on a station or in application of the fairness doctrine. He said the FCC action, coming during a Washington convention of the National Association of Broadcasters (NAB), constituted "intimidation," and a step toward "censorship."

The FCC said an administrative law judge, with subpoena powers, would conduct the probe. Stations could be charged under federal law banning the broadcast of "obscene, indecent or profane material," or could be subject to early hearings on license renewal.

Burch told the NAB convention March 28 that if broadcasters allowed themselves to "cop out" of their "responsibilities" to remove obscene programming, they would "end up paying the price for a handful" of broadcasters.

FCC ordered to lift cable TV obscenity rule. The U.S. Court of Appeals for the District of Columbia Sept. 1, 1977 ordered the FCC to suspend a rule requiring cable television operators to prescreen and censor "obscene or indecent matter." The order had been sought by the American Civil Liberties Union (ACLU), which contended that the regulation violated the First Amendment.

The matter was remanded to the FCC, which indicated it would revise or repeal the regulation. A spokesman for the National Cable Television Association noted that with or without the FCC regulation cable operators were still bound by local criminal statutes governing the transmission of obscene material.

Penn radio loses license. Walter C. Miller, an FCC administrative law judge, ordered the FCC April 4, 1977 not to renew the license of the University of Pennsylvania radio station. Miller, who had conducted a license-renewal hearing for the station, WXPN-FM of Philadelphia, said the student operators had broadcast "sordid utterances of the most vile type."

The station had received a warning from the FCC in 1976, following a number of complaints about its programs. Miller criticized university officials for allowing "licentious slime and nauseating verbiage" to be broadcast even after the school had been warned.

Miller cited other WXPN violations of FCC rules, including the use of hashish, marijuana and alcohol on the station premises and operating at times without a properly licensed engineer.

'Filthy words' ban upheld. The Supreme Court ruled, 5–4, July 3, 1978 that the FCC could ban the broadcast of language that was not legally obscene. The case was *FCC v. Pacifica Foundation.*

The case involved a portion of a record album by comedian George Carlin broadcast over the radio in 1973 by WBAI-FM, the New York City station of the Pacifica Foundation. In the 12-minute monologue, entitled "Filthy Words," Carlin discussed seven words "you couldn't say on the public airwaves . . . shit, piss, fuck, cunt, cocksucker, motherfucker and tits. Those are the ones that will curve your spine, grow hair on your hands and maybe bring us, God help us, peace without honor."

A motorist subsequently complained to the FCC that his young son had heard the broadcast, which had played at 2 p.m. The FCC reprimanded WBAI, though the agency indicated that the broadcast might have been permissible late at night, when children were less likely to be listening.

Pacifica challenged the reprimand in court, arguing that the FCC's action violated the First Amendment. The foundation claimed that the monologue was not legally obscene under constitutional interpretations. (The current legal doctrine said that material was obscene if it offended community standards and lacked "serious literary, artistic, political or scientific value.")

The station won its case in the U.S. Court of Appeals for the District of Columbia. The Supreme Court reversed the appeals court. Writing for the majority, Justice John Paul Stevens held that "patently offensive, indecent material presented over the airwaves confronts the citizen, not only in public, but also in the privacy of the home, where the individual's right to be let alone plainly outweighs the First Amendment rights of the intruder."

Stevens noted that the FCC was empowered by Congress to curb the broadcast of "obscene, indecent or profane language." The FCC, he said, was free to conclude that language was "indecent," even though it lacked "prurient appeal. . . . We hold simply that when the commission finds that a pig has entered the parlor, the exercise of its regulatory power doesn't depend on proof that the pig is obscene."

Stevens stressed that the majority was taking a narrow stand on the issue. He suggested that "an occasional expletive" broadcast over the airwaves would not justify FCC sanctions.

In dissent, Justice Potter Stewart backed the Pacifica argument that the Carlin monologue was not "obscene" in the legal sense of the word. Stewart was joined by Justices William J. Brennan Jr., Byron R. White and Thurgood Marshall.

Brennan and Marshall issued a separate dissent objecting to the majority's stand that broadcasts had only limited First Amendment protection because they went into the home. Brennan said that the stand permitted "majoritarian tastes" to dictate the content of broadcasts.

The ruling was generally criticized by the broadcasting industry, which had joined the Justice Department in support of Pacifica.

FCC rejects censorship role—Federal Communications Commission Chairman Charles D. Ferris assured the broadcasting industry July 21 that the FCC was "not going to become a censor" as the result of a July 3 Supreme Court decision.

Ferris, in a speech to the New England Broadcasting Association in Boston, said that commentators were mistaken if they read "the court's decision as a signal to the FCC to stifle nonconforming speech." The FCC, he maintained, was "far more dedicated to the First Amendment premises that broadcasters should air controversial programming" than it was "worried about an occasional four-letter word."

As an example of the FCC's policy, Ferris cited the agency's decision July 20 to renew the license of WGBH, Boston's public television station. The renewal had been challenged by Morality in Media, a national anti-pornography organization. The group had charged in a petition to the FCC that WGBH's programming contained nudity and "vulgar material."

Ferris told his audience that although he might feel comfortable deciding for himself what constituted "accepted standards of moralty" or "patently offensive speech," he would not "feel comfortable making those decisions for others."

Obscenity in the Mail

Nixon urges ban on mailed obscenity. In a message to Congress May 2, 1969, President Richard M. Nixon had proposed new legislation to restrict the mailing of obscene material. Congress, however, failed to complete action on the Administration's bills, and they died when Congress adjourned in 1970.

President Nixon asked for three new laws to halt the flow of obscene mail. "American homes," the President said, "are being bombarded with the largest volume of sex-oriented mail in history" and said most of it "is unsolicited, unwanted and deeply offensive to those who receive it." He proposed:

(a) A law against use of the mails or other facilities of commerce, to deliver to anyone under 18 material dealing with a sexual subject in a manner unsuitable for young people, (b) a statute to bar the mails for the commercial exploitation of a prurient interest in sex through advertising, (c) expansion of a 1967 law to enable a citizen to protect his home from any intrusion of sex-oriented advertising. (A three-judge federal panel April 30 upheld the constitutionality of the 1967 law, and a three-judge federal panel ruled Sept. 9, 1969 in Atlanta that a law allowing the postmaster general to stop mail deliveries to suspected vendors of obscene material was unconstitutional.)

The House July 7, 1971, voted, 356 to 25, to ban the sending of obscene material through the mail, but the Senate took no action on the proposal.

Mailing conviction upheld. The Supreme Court June 24, 1974 upheld the obscenity conviction of six Los Angeles men for the mailing of obscene material—a brochure advertising the "illustrated presidential report on the commission on obscenity and pornography."

The material that they mailed showed sexual acts and behavior forbidden under the 1973 guidelines. According to the U.S. 9th Circuit Court of Appeals, which affirmed the convictions, the brochure had pictures of "heterosexual and homosexual intercourse, sodomy and a variety of deviate sexual acts." The original trial jury had been unable to decide whether the book itself was obscene.

Child Pornography

Wide pornographic abuse of children. In 1977 investigative media reports, local law enforcement data and congressional hearings pointed to the existence of a nationwide multi-million-dollar pornography and prostitution industry based upon the sexual exploitation of children. The child pornography network reportedly involved more than 300,000 children under 16 years of age and was thought to be increasingly under the influence of organized crime.

The so-called kiddie porn operation was headquartered in Los Angeles. Los Angeles police sergeant Lloyd Martin, head of a special police unit on child abuse assigned to the problem, was interviewed on CBS television's "60 Minutes" broadcast May 15. He described the extensive procurement and prostitution of children, predominantly young boys, some as young as three years old.

Los Angeles deputy police chief Daryl Gates told the House Select Committee on Education and Labor May 27 that previous reports that 30,000 children in Los Angeles alone were involved in pornography was "probably a very conservative figure."

According to Martin, runaways from around the country congregated in an area of Hollywood known as "The Meat Rack" where pederasts, commonly called "chicken hawks," picked them up. The chicken hawk, who was often also a pornographer, would offer a homeless youth money or sometimes just a meal to pose for photographs. (Pederasty is sexual relations between a man and a boy.)

The pictures, depicting children in explicit sexual acts with each other or with adults, were sold to pornographic magazines that retailed for five to ten dollars a copy at so-called adult bookstores. An eight millimeter kiddie pornographic film cost as much as $50 a reel.

Incest, in addition to pedophilia, was a popular theme in underground sex publications. Incestuous parents often volunteered or sold their own children to pornographers after abusing them themselves.

Similar sexual exploitation was carried out with children recruited from foster care programs, institutions for the mentally retarded, summer camps and modeling agencies.

A four-part series on child pornography published by the Chicago Tribune May 15–18 described several illicit child abuse schemes. In Winchester, Tenn. an Episcopal priest, the Rev. Claudius Ira Vermilye Jr., 47, was arrested on charges of staging homosexual orgies and filming them at Boys Farm Inc. The refuge for wayward teenagers was allegedly a front for the production of pornographic films that were distributed to the "charity's" so-called "donors," who were located throughout the country. The farm had been subsidized by state and county funds.

A total of 19 men were charged April 11 in New Orleans with multiple counts of crimes against nature in a case involving a now-defunct Boy Scout troop that had been allegedly organized in 1974 for the express purpose of sexually abusing young boys. New Orleans Detective Mason Spong told Chicago Tribune reporters George Bliss and Michael Sneed that the investigation into the troop's activities extended into 34 states.

The reporters also named John D. Norman, a convicted sodomist currently serving a four-year prison term, as the mastermind of the Delta Project, a homosexual ring that trafficked in young boys. The group, based in Chicago, allegedly supplied boy prostitutes to pederasts throughout the U.S. Police in Dallas, Tex. reportedly had linked Norman to the ring implicated in the 1973 sex and sadism case in which 27 boys were murdered.

The reporters' three-month investigation also uncovered the kiddie porn newsletter "Hermes," which had a circulation of more than 5,000. The bimonthly publication, which sold at $10 a copy, grossed over $330,000 a year.

A seven-month investigation by the Manhattan (N.Y.) District Attorney's office led to the arrest April 26 of eight alleged pornographers. Detectives confiscated 4,000 prints of films showing children between eight and 12 years of age engaged in explicit sex.

Legal system inadequate—Such commercial sex ventures were able to flourish because of inadequacies in the legal system. Law enforcement officials often could not prosecute pornographers because appropriate laws did not exist. In Illinois, the state's obscenity law had been declared unconstitutional by a federal court in June 1976.

Chicago's Acting Mayor Michael Bilandic May 20 tried to use the city's building ordinance to close down 34 pornographic bookshops, but a federal judge ruled that it was unconstitutional to "fight obscenity by any actions under the building code."

Congressional hearings into proposed federal legislation against child pornography focused attention on how the producers and distributors of such material were protected under the Constitution's First Amendment guarantee of free expression. Previous attempts to legally define what was obscene had failed and invariably raised the question of censorship.

Dr. Judianne Densen-Gerber, a psychiatrist who headed Odyssey House, a New York City establishment for troubled youth, had campaigned around the country for legislation that would stop the abuse of minors. She testified May 23 before the House Judiciary subcommittee on crime that, "If I had to give up a portion of my First Amendment rights to stop this stuff [child pornography], then I'd be willing to do it."

Child porn increasing. *Time* magazine reported in its April 4, 1977 issue that, "according to police in Los Angeles, New York and Chicago, sales [of child pornography] began to surge a year or two ago and are still climbing." State's Attorney Bernard Carey of Cook County is cited as reporting that "porno pictures of children as young as five and six are now generally available throughout Chicago."

Time reported these "recent developments": "Underground sex magazines are heavily stressing incest and pedophilia. . . . In San Francisco hard-core child-porn films were shown in a moviehouse for five weeks before police seized the films last February. . . . Until recently, much child porn sold in America was smuggled in from abroad. Now most of it appears to be home grown. . . . "

The Washington Star quoted an explanation by Robert Kendall, Justice Department attorney specializing in obscenity prosecution, for the escalation of pornography: "Just a few years ago, it was straight sex between couples. Then we escalated to explicit ejaculation, then groups of three and four people, then bisexuality, S&M, bestiality, urination and defecation, then snuff. Now we're going through a very bad stage. Children. In order for pornography to survive, there must be a new product. They'll do anything to make that almighty buck."

A statement by the Odyssey Institute of New York reports that "by recent count, there are at least 264 different magazines being sold in adult bookstores across the country dealing with sexual acts between children or between children and adults. . . . Film makers and magazine photographers have little difficulty recruiting youngsters for these performances. Some simply use their own children; others rely on runaways. . . ."

Child porn curbs enacted. Congress Jan. 24, 1978 completed action on a bill making the interstate use of children for prostitution or for the production of pornographic materials a federal crime. The legislation came in response to reports in 1977 of widespread sexual exploitation of children. President Jimmy Carter signed the measure, the Protection of Children Against Sexual Exploitation Act of 1977, Feb. 6, 1978.

In its major provisions, the bill:

■ Made it a crime to have any child under age 16 engage in sexually explicit conduct for the purpose of producing material for interstate commerce. A parent or guardian who knowingly allowed such activity would be liable to prosecution.

■ Barred the sale or distribution of obscene material showing children engaged in sexually explicit conduct, provided the material had been in interstate commerce.

■ Outlawed interstate transportation of males and females under the age of 18 for the purposes of prostitution or other sexual commerce.

Other Developments

W. Va. textbook protesters convicted. A federal jury in Charleston, W. Va. April 18, 1975 found Marvin Horan, a self-ordained fundamentalist minister, and Larry Elmer Stevens, a coal miner, guilty in connection with the bombing of public schools there during the height of the Kanawah County textbook protests in the fall of 1974.

Stevens, described by prosecutors as Horan's right-hand man, was found guilty of the six counts with which he had been charged—conspiracy to bomb, possession of dynamite, manufacture of the bombs and the bombings themselves.

Horan was convicted of one count of conspiracy to bomb the schools, but he was acquitted of three related counts.

Two other defendants, Delbert Lee Rose and Wayne Blankenship, were allowed to plead guilty to lesser charges when they agreed to be witnesses for the prosecution.

In a related development, an eight-member National Education Association (NEA) investigative panel said in an 87-page report made public Feb. 6 that infiltration of the protest movement by "highly sophisticated, well organized, right-wing extremist groups" made the Kanawah County textbook dispute longer and more violent than it otherwise would have been. While some money to support the protest came from individual donors, the report said, other aid came from extreme right groups associated with or in sympathy with the John Birch Society. Among these were the Los Angeles-based Citizens for Decency Through Law, the Birch Society-affiliated American Opinion book store in Reedy, W. Va., the Heritage Foundation, Inc. of Washington and Mr. and Mrs. Mel Gabler, of Longview, Tex., whom the report called "self-appointed textbook censors."

The NEA study was also critical of the Kanawah County school board for failing to communicate effectively with rural parents, failing to see an earlier dispute over sex education as a warning, failing to consult parents before adopting disputed textbooks and failing to have a policy for dealing with challenges and disputes over textbooks.

The dispute involved some 325 new textbooks purchased for the county schools. After months of argument, picketing and marches had begun in earnest as school opened Sept. 3, 1974. The protests brought boycotts, school closings and wildcat strikes by coal miners.

The protests, led by fundamentalist ministers, opposed supplementary English texts alleged by protesters to be obscene, blasphemous and anti-American. The original crusade to have the books withdrawn had been led by Mrs. Alice Moore, a member of the county board of education, who contended that the books interfered with parental authority and could destroy the conservative religious and moral values prevalent in the area.

(The texts reportedly contained sections dealing with controversial "modern" issues such as drugs, sex, family relationships, race and radicalism.)

Some 8,000 coal miners in a four-county area staged their strikes as school opened as part of an effort described by one fundamentalist minister as complete disruption of both education and business in the area to put pressure on the school board. The walkouts were not sanctioned by the United Mine Workers leadership. Sympathy school boycotts and demonstrations in three counties adjoining Kanawha resulted in sporadic school closings.

A compromise agreement between protesters and the board was negotiated during the second week of demonstrations under which 90% of the disputed texts would be removed and all would be subjected to a review by an 18-member citizens' panel. Some leaders, however, continued demands for complete and final withdrawal of all the materials.

Although a circuit court judge had issued an anti-picketing injunction Sept. 5, demonstrations continued after the compromise accord; the number of protesters, however had fallen markedly by Sept. 20. One defusing aspect was the arrest of 11 demonstrators Sept. 18, including three of the ministers. The ministers were jailed and fined for violating the injunction. By Sept. 20 about half of the striking miners were reported back at work.

The board, which had removed the books 40 days earlier, decided Nov. 8 to reinstate all but seven of them. However, in a conciliatory gesture, it passed resolutions excusing students from using books they or their parents found morally or religiously "objectionable," and forbidding teachers to "indoctrinate" students in objectionable moral or religious "values."

The vote on the books was 4-1. Mrs. Alice Moore, the conservative board member who led the anti-book fight, said almost all of the new textbooks contained selections she found "vulgar, profane, violent, critical of parents, depressing, seditious, revolutionary, anti-Christian and immoral."

Several elementary schools were dynamited or firebombed during October, and the building which housed offices of the school board was bombed Oct. 30. Physical damage was caused in each case. An automobile belonging to a family which defied the school boycott was blown up Nov. 11.

The continuing controversy drew its first policy statement from the Ford Administration Dec. 2, in a speech by U.S. Education Commissioner Terrel H. Bell. Bell told a meeting of the School Division of the Association of American Publishers that schoolbook publishers should print "good literature that will appeal to children without relying too much on blood and guts and street language," and said they should "chart a middle course between the scholar's legitimate claim to academic freedom in presenting new knowledge and social commentary on the one hand, and the legitimate expectation of parents that schools will respect their moral and ethical values on the other."

Bell's statement was denounced Dec. 2 by Paul B. Salmon, executive director of the American Association of School Administrators, who asserted it fanned the flames of various schoolbook controversies around the nation.

Before the anti-book demonstration in Charleston, the Kanawha County School Board had adopted guidelines for the selection of future textbooks. The guidelines had been proposed in their initial form by Alice Moore, a leader of the anti-book movement.

The board voted Nov. 21 to establish four screening committees for the selection of books for social studies, music, business education and home economics in April 1975. Each committee would have five teachers and 15 parents, and would use the following criteria in selecting books:

The books must respect the privacy of students' homes, not asking personal questions and not encouraging students to criticize their parents; they must not contain offensive language and they must not ridicule the values and practices of any ethnic, religious or racial group, or encourage racial hatred; they must not encourage sedition or revolution against the U.S. government, or teach that an alien form of government was superior; textbooks used to study the English language must teach traditional rules of grammar.

There were also textbook disputes in other parts of the U.S. Among them:

Community pressure in Pierceton, Ind. forced the local school board Nov. 20 to outlaw an English textbook series which contained profanity and selections from the writings of Eldridge Cleaver, the black militant, and Woody Guthrie, the folk singer. Pupils could read the books as electives if they had parental permission.

Economy Co. of Oklahoma Nov. 23 filed a $30 million libel, slander and conspiracy suit against three women who had successfully opposed approval of the use of its textbooks in the Texas public schools. The Texas Board of Education had voted unanimously Nov. 9 to remove the Economy readers from textbook lists already approved by the commissioner of education and the state textbook committee. It was the first such action in Texas history.

Hustler publisher convicted of obscenity. Larry C. Flynt, publisher and executive editor of *Hustler* magazine, was found guilty in Cincinnati Feb. 8, 1977 of obscenity and of engaging in organized crime. Hamilton County Common Pleas Court Judge William J. Morrissey sentenced Flynt to concurrent sentences of seven to 25 years in prison and a $10,000 fine—the maximum sentence for an organized crime conviction—and six months in the county jail and a $1,000 fine on the obscenity charge.

In addition, Hustler Magazine Inc., of which Flynt was president, was fined $10,-000 for engaging in organized crime and $1,000 for pandering obscenity. (Under Ohio law, corporations were treated as individuals.)

The organized crime charges were based on a 1974 state law that made liable for prosecution five or more individuals who engaged in illegal activity for profit.

Hustler, with a monthly circulation of about two million, ranked behind Playboy

and Penthouse as the best-selling national men's magazine. It was regarded as one of the most explicit of the commercial sex publications.

The jury of seven men and five women had an average age in the mid-40s, and most came from blue-collar backgrounds. Many were reported to have shown discomfort during the presentation of evidence against the magazine. That evidence had included stories from Hustler detailing incest, bestiality, sadism and other sexual practices considered deviate. The prosecution also displayed photos of nude women—including Flynt's wife, Althea Leasure—that had appeared in the magazine.

(Flynt's wife, Althea; his brother, Jimmy, and Al Van Schaik, all officers of Hustler Magazine Inc., were acquitted of organized crime and pandering obscenity charges.)

Judge Morrissey had refused to allow the defense to admit as evidence other men's magazines sold in Hamilton County. Flynt's defense team had attempted to contend that since a number of sex publications were available in the area, Hustler could not be singled out for violating community standards on obscenity.

The defense also challenged Hamilton County's jurisdiction over the editorial and production operations of the magazine. Hustler's editorial offices were in Columbus, Ohio (Franklin County), it was printed in Milwaukee, Wis. and distributed out of Connecticut. Hamilton County prosecutor Simon L. Leis Jr. refuted that argument by saying the defendants had "aided and abetted" the Marshall News Co., the magazine's local distributor. The company had been named as an unindicted co-conspirator in the case.

Following Flynt's sentencing, Leis said that "a moral boundary has been established in this county as well as this country. Americans will put limitations on how far smut peddlers will go."

Flynt was taken immediately to the county jail. The Court of Appeals of the First Appellate District of Ohio Feb. 14 ordered him released on $50,000 bond pending appeal.

Flynt shot—Larry Flynt was shot March 6, 1978 on a street in Lawrenceville, Ga. He was critically injured.

At the time of the shooting, he was returning with his lawyer (who was also wounded) to the state court where he had been testifying at his own trial. Flynt had been charged with distributing obscene material.

In two operations doctors removed his spleen and parts of his intestine. Flynt was a vegetarian and fruitarian who had, according to his custom, had two enemas the day prior to the shooting and had fasted approximately 24 hours. This had increased his chances for survival, the doctors said, as it reduced the danger of infection.

A third operation was performed to remove what was reported to be a .44-cal. magnum bullet and bone chips from his spinal cord. Flynt was left paralyzed from the waist down.

The Kentucky-born Flynt had been active in Georgia (buying The Plains Monitor in President Carter's hometown and The Gazette in Atlanta) since becoming a "born again Christian". He attributed his conversion in late 1977 to Ruth Stapleton, the President's sister.

Earlier on the day he was shot, Flynt had said on the witness stand that his magazine offended his principles but he did not consider it illegal. He added "I feel drinking is wrong, but it's not illegal."

After the shooting, the judge announced a mistrial and dismissed the jury.

Maryland provision invalid. The Supreme Court April 24, 1978 upheld, by refusing to review, a decision of the Maryland Court of Appeals striking down portions of the state's obscenity law. The provision had allowed the state to prosecute clerks in adult book stores while exempting from prosecution employees of theaters showing films judged to be obscene. The case was *Maryland v. Wheeler.*

The Significant
Court Decisions

Public action on the issue of pornography and obscenity depends on law—and on what the courts determine to be law. Both law and the courts' interpretation of law change with time. Several court decisions are important to an understanding of the legal status of pornography and obscenity in the 1970s. These findings probably begin with the 1933 ruling that authorized the importation of James Joyce's novel Ulysses. The Ulysses *opinion and other court decisions of significance to this issue follow (either in full or abridged).*

Ulysses Found Not Obscene

A landmark ruling on the issue of pornography was rendered by Federal Judge John Woolsey in U.S. District Court in New York Dec. 6, 1933. Woolsey ruled (a) that James Joyce's novel Ulysses *was "not pornographic" and therefore could be legally imported into the United States, (b) that judgment of a book under obscenity rules should be based on the book "in its entirety" and (c) that judgment of the book's tendency to stir sex impulses should be tested by opinion as to the book's "effect on a person with average sex instincts." Woolsey's opinion in the case of* United States v. One Book Called "Ulysses" *follows.*

The motion for a decree dismissing the libel herein is granted, and, consequently, of course, the Government's motion for a decree of forfeiture and destruction is denied.

Accordingly a decree dismissing the libel without costs may be entered herein.

I. The practice followed in this case is in accordance with the suggestion made by me in the case of *United States v. One Book Entitled "Contraception,"* and is as follows:

After issue was joined by the filing of the claimant's answer to the libel for forfeiture against "Ulysses," a stipulation was made between the United States Attorney's office and the attorneys for the claimant providing:

1. That the book "Ulysses" should be deemed to have been annexed to and to have become part of the libel just as if it had been incorporated in its entirety therein.

2. That the parties waived their right to a trial by jury.

3. That each party agreed to move for decree in its favor.

4. That on such cross motions the Court might decide all the questions of law and fact involved and render a general finding thereon.

5. That on the decision of such motions the decree of the Court might be entered as if it were a decree after trial.

It seems to me that a procedure of this kind is highly appropriate in libels for the confiscation of books such as this. It is an especially advantageous procedure in the instant case because on account of the length of "Ulysses" and the difficulty of reading it, a jury trial would have been an extremely unsatisfactory, if not an almost impossible, method of dealing with it.

II. I have read "Ulysses" once in its entirety and I have read those passages of which the Government particularly complains several times. In fact, for many weeks, my spare time has been devoted to the consideration of the decision which my duty would require me to make in this matter.

"Ulysses" is not an easy book to read or to understand. But there has been much written about it, and in order properly to approach the consideration of it it is advisable to read a number of other books which have now become its satellites. The study of "Ulysses" is, therefore, a heavy task.

III. The reputation of "Ulysses" in the literary world, however, warranted my taking such time as was necessary to enable me to satisfy myself as to the intent with which the book was written, for, of course, in any case where a book is claimed to be obscene it must first be determined whether the intent with which it was written was what is called, according to the usual phrase, pornographic—that is, written for the purpose of exploiting obscenity.

If the conclusion is that the book is pornographic that is the end of the inquiry and forfeiture must follow.

But in "Ulysses," in spite of its unusual frankness, I do not detect anywhere the leer of the sensualist. I hold, therefore, that it is not pornographic.

IV. In writing "Ulysses," Joyce sought to make a serious experiment in a new, if not wholly novel, literary genre. He takes persons of the lower middle class living in Dublin in 1904 and seeks not only to describe what they did on a certain day early in June of that year as they went about the City bent on their usual occupations, but also to tell what many of them thought about the while.

Joyce has attempted—it seems to me, with astonishing success—to show how the screen of consciousness with its evershifting kaleidoscopic impressions carries, as it were on a plastic palimpsest, not only what is in the focus of each man's observation of the actual things about him, but also in a penumbral zone residua of past impressions, some recent and some drawn up by association from the domain of the subconscious. He shows how each of these impressions affect the life and behavior of the character which he is describing.

What he seeks to get is not unlike the result of a double or, if that is possible, a multiple exposure on a cinema film which would give a clear foreground with a background visible but somewhat blurred and out of focus in varying degrees.

To convey by words an effect which obviously lends itself more appropriately to a graphic technique, accounts, it seems to me, for much of the obscurity which meets a reader of "Ulysses." And it also explains another aspect of the book, which I have further to consider, namely, Joyce's sincerity and his honest effort to show exactly how the minds of his characters operate.

If Joyce did not attempt to be honest in developing the technique which he has adopted in "Ulysses" the result would be psychologically misleading and thus unfaithful to his chosen technique. Such an attitude would be artistically inexcusable.

It is because Joyce has been loyal to his technique and has not funked its necessary implications, but has honestly attempted to tell fully what his characters think about, that he has been the subject of so many attacks and that his purpose has been so often misunderstood and misrepresented. For his attempt sincerely and honestly to realize his objective has required him incidentally to use certain words which are generally considered dirty words and has led at times to what many think is a too poignant preoccupation with sex in the thought of his characters.

The words which are criticized as dirty are old Saxon words known to almost all men and, I venture, to many women, and are such words as would be naturally and habitually used, I believe, by the types of folk whose life, physical and mental, Joyce is seeking to describe. In respect of the recurrent emergence of the theme of sex in the minds of his characters, it must always be remembered that his locale was Celtic and his season Spring.

Whether or not one enjoys such a technique as Joyce uses is a matter of taste on which disagreement or argument is futile, but to subject that technique to the standards of some other technique seems to me to be little short of absurd.

Accordingly, I hold that "Ulysses" is a sincere and honest book and I think that the criticisms of it are entirely disposed of by its rationale.

V. Furthermore, "Ulysses" is an amazing *tour de force* when one considers the success which has been in the main achieved with such a difficult objective as Joyce set for himself. As I have stated, "Ulysses" is not an easy book to read. It is brilliant and dull, intelligible and obscure by turns. In many places it seems to me to be disgusting, but although it contains, as I have mentioned above, many words usually considered dirty, I have not found any thing that I consider to be dirt for dirt's sake. Each word of the book contributes like a bit of mosaic to the detail of the picture which Joyce is seeking to construct for his readers.

If one does not wish to associate with such folk as Joyce describes, that is one's own choice. In order to avoid indirect contact with them one may not wish to read "Ulysses"; that is quite understandable. But when such a real artist in words, as Joyce undoubtedly is, seeks to draw a true picture of the lower middle class in a European city, ought it to be impossible for the American public legally to see that picture?

To answer this question it is not sufficient merely to find, as I have found above, that Joyce did not write "Ulysses" with what is commonly called pornographic intent, I must endeavor to apply a more objective standard to his book in order to determine its effect in the result, irrespective of the intent with which it was written.

VI. The statute under which the libel is filed only denounces, in so far as we are here concerned, the importation into the United States from any foreign country of "any obscene book." Section 305 of the Tariff Act of 1930, Title 19 United States Code, Section 1305. It does not marshal against books the spectrum of condemnatory adjectives found, commonly, in laws dealing with matters of this kind. I am, therefore, only required to determine whether "Ulysses" is obscene within the legal definition of that word.

The meaning of the word "obscene" as legally defined by the Courts is: tending to stir the sex impulses or to lead to sexually impure and lustful thoughts. . . .

Whether a particular book would tend to excite such impulses and thoughts must be tested by the Court's opinion as to its effect on a person with average sex instincts—what the French would call *l'homme moyen sensuel*—who plays, in this branch of legal inquiry, the same role of hypothetical reagent as does the "reasonable man" in the law of torts and "the man learned in the art" on questions of invention in patent law.

The risk involved in the use of such a reagent arises from the inherent tendency of the trier of facts, however fair he may intend to be, to make his reagent too much subservient to his own idiosyncrasies. Here, I have attempted to avoid this, if possible, and to make my reagent herein more objective than he might otherwise be, by adopting the following course:

After I had made my decision in regard to the aspect of "Ulysses," now under consideration, I checked my impressions with two friends of mine who in my opinion answered to the above stated requirement for my reagent.

These literary assessors—as I might properly describe them—were called on separately, and neither knew that I was consulting the other. They are men whose opinion on literature and on life I value most highly. They had both read "Ulysses," and, of course, were wholly unconnected with this cause.

Without letting either of my assessors know what my decision was, I gave to each of them the legal definition of obscene and asked each whether in his opinion "Ulysses" was obscene within that definition.

I was interested to find that they both agreed with my opinion: that reading "Ulysses" in its entirety, as a book must be read on

such a test as this, did not tend to excite sexual impulses or lustful thoughts but that its net effect on them was only that of a
somewhat tragic and very powerful commentary on the inner
lives of men and women.

It is only with the normal person that the law is concerned.
Such a test as I have described, therefore, is the only proper test
of obscenity in the case of a book like "Ulysses" which is a sincere and serious attempt to devise a new literary method for the
observation and description of mankind.

I am quite aware that owing to some of its scenes "Ulysses"
is a rather strong draught to ask some sensitive, though normal,
persons to take. But my considered opinion, after long reflec-
tion, is that whilst in many places the effect of "Ulysses" on the
reader undoubtedly is somewhat emetic, nowhere does it tend to
be an aphrodisiac.

"Ulysses" may, therefore, be admitted into the United
States.

Roth & Alberts Cases: No First Amendment Protection
for Obscenity; Community Standards Become Criterion

In an opinion rendered jointly on two cases, Roth
v. United States *and* Alberts v. California, *the
U.S. Supreme Court ruled June 27, 1957 that obscenity was not a form of expression protected by
the First Amendment's guarantee of free speech
and press. It also provided new criteria—including "contemporary community standards"—as a
test for judging whether material is obscene. The
decision upheld the convictions of two defendants
in obscenity cases. The majority opinion, written
by Justice William J. Brennan, follows.*

The constitutionality of a criminal obscenity statute is the
question in each of these cases. In *Roth,* the primary constitutional question is whether the federal obscenity statute violates
the provision of the First Amendment that "Congress shall
make no law . . . abridging the freedom of speech, or of the
press. . . ." In *Alberts,* the primary constitutional question is
whether the obscenity provisions of the California Penal Code
invade the freedoms of speech and press as they may be incor-

porated in the liberty protected from state action by the Due Process Clause of the Fourteenth Amendment.

Other constitutional questions are: whether these statutes violate due process, because too vague to support conviction for crime; whether power to punish speech and press offensive to decency and morality is in the States alone, so that the federal obscenity statute violates the Ninth and Tenth Amendments (raised in *Roth*); and whether Congress, by enacting the federal obscenity statute, under the power delegated by Art. I, § 8, cl. 7, to establish post offices and post roads, pre-empted the regulation of the subject matter (raised in *Alberts*).

Roth conducted a business in New York in the publication and sale of books, photographs and magazines. He used circulars and advertising matter to solicit sales. He was convicted by a jury in the District Court for the Southern District of New York upon 4 counts of a 26-count indictment charging him with mailing obscene circulars and advertising, and an obscene book, in violation of the federal obscenity statute. His conviction was affirmed by the Court of Appeals for the Second Circuit. We granted certiorari.

Alberts conducted a mail-order business from Los Angeles. He was convicted by the Judge of the Municipal Court of the Beverly Hills Judicial District (having waived a jury trial) under a misdemeanor complaint which charged him with lewdly keeping for sale obscene and indecent books, and with writing, composing and publishing an obscene advertisement of them, in violation of the California Penal Code. The conviction was affirmed by the Appellate Department of the Superior Court of the State of California in and for the County of Los Angeles. We noted probable jurisdiction.

The dispositive question is whether obscenity is utterance within the area of protected speech and press. Although this is the first time the question has been squarely presented to this Court, either under the First Amendment or under the Fourteenth Amendment, expressions found in numerous opinions indicate that this Court has always assumed that obscenity is not protected by the freedoms of speech and press. . . .

The guaranties of freedom of expression in effect in 10 of the 14 States which by 1792 had ratified the Constitution, gave no absolute protection for every utterance. Thirteen of the 14 States provided for the prosecution of libel, and all of those States made either blasphemy or profanity, or both, statutory

crimes. As early as 1712, Massachusetts made it criminal to publish "any filthy, obscene, or profane song, pamphlet, libel or
mock sermon" in imitation or mimicking of religious services. . . . Thus, profanity and obscenity were related
offenses.

In light of this history, it is apparent that the unconditional
phrasing of the First Amendment was not intended to protect every utterance. This phrasing did not prevent this Court from
concluding that libelous utterances are not within the area of
constitutionally protected speech. . . . At the time of the adoption of the First Amendment, obscenity law was not as fully developed as libel law, but there is sufficiently contemporaneous
evidence to show that obscenity, too, was outside the protection
intended for speech and press.

The protection given speech and press was fashioned to assure unfettered interchange of ideas for the bringing about of political and social changes desired by the people. This objective
was made explicit as early as 1774 in a letter of the Continental
Congress to the inhabitants of Quebec:

"The last right we shall mention, regards the freedom of the
press. The importance of this consists, besides the advancement
of truth, science, morality, and arts in general, in its diffusion of
liberal sentiments on the administration of Government, its
ready communication of thoughts between subjects, and its
consequential promotion of union among them, whereby oppressive officers are shamed or intimidated, into more honoura-
ble and just modes of conducting affairs." . . .

All ideas having even the slightest redeeming social importance—unorthodox ideas, controversial ideas, even ideas hateful to the prevailing climate of opinion—have the full protection
of the guaranties, unless excludable because they encroach upon
the limited area of more important interests. But implicit in the
history of the First Amendment is the rejection of obscenity as
utterly without redeeming social importance. This rejection for
that reason is mirrored in the universal judgment that obscenity
should be restrained, reflected in the international agreement of
over 50 nations, in the obscenity laws of all the 48 States, and in
the 20 obscenity laws enacted by Congress from 1842 to 1956.
This is the same judgment expressed by this Court in *Chaplinsky
v. New Hampshire* . . . :

". . . There are certain well-defined and narrowly limited
classes of speech, the prevention and punishment of which have

never been thought to raise any Constitutional problem. *These include the lewd and obscene. . . . It has been well observed that such utterances are no essential part of any exposition of ideas, and are of such slight social value as a step to truth that any benefit that may be derived from them is clearly outweighed by the social interest in order and morality. . . .*" (Emphasis added.)

We hold that obscenity is not within the area of constitutionally protected speech or press.

It is strenuously urged that these obscenity statutes offend the constitutional guaranties because they punish incitation to impure sexual *thoughts,* not shown to be related to any overt antisocial conduct which is or may be incited in the persons stimulated to such *thoughts.* In *Roth,* the trial judge instructed the jury: "The words 'obscene, lewd and lascivious' as used in the law, signify that form of immorality which has relation to sexual impurity and has a tendency to excite lustful *thoughts.*" (Emphasis added.) In *Alberts,* the trial judge applied the test laid down in *People v. Wepplo . . .* namely, whether the material has "a substantial tendency to deprave or corrupt its readers by inciting lascivious *thoughts* or arousing lustful desires." (Emphasis added.) It is insisted that the constitutional guaranties are violated because convictions may be had without proof either that obscene material will perceptibly create a clear and present danger of antisocial conduct, or will probably induce its recipients to such conduct. But, in light of our holding that obscenity is not protected speech, the complete answer to this argument is in the holding of this Court in *Beauharnais v. Illinois . . . :*

"Libelous utterances not being within the area of constitutionally protected speech, it is unnecessary, either for us or for the State courts, to consider the issues behind the phrase 'clear and present danger.' Certainly no one would contend that obscene speech, for example, may be punished only upon a showing of such circumstances. Libel, as we have seen, is in the same class."

However, sex and obscenity are not synonymous. Obscene material is material which deals with sex in a manner appealing to prurient interest. The portrayal of sex, *e. g.,* in art, literature and scientific works, is not itself sufficient reason to deny material the constitutional protection of freedom of speech and press. Sex, a great and mysterious motive force in human life, has indisputably been a subject of absorbing interest to mankind through the ages; it is one of the vital problems of human interest and public concern. As to all such problems, this Court said in *Thornhill v. Alabama* . . . :

"The freedom of speech and of the press guaranteed by the Constitution embraces at the least the liberty to discuss publicly and truthfully *all matters of public concern* without previous restraint or fear of subsequent punishment. The exigencies of the colonial period and the efforts to secure freedom from oppressive administration developed a broadened conception of these liberties as adequate to supply the public need for *information and education with respect to the significant issues of the times.* . . . Freedom of discussion, if it would fulfill its historic function in this nation, must embrace *all issues about which information is needed or appropriate to enable the members of society to cope with the exigencies of their period.*" (Emphasis added.)

The fundamental freedoms of speech and press have contributed greatly to the development and well-being of our free society and are indispensable to its continued growth. Ceaseless vigilance is the watchword to prevent their erosion by Congress or by the States. The door barring federal and state intrusion into this area cannot be left ajar; it must be kept tightly closed and opened only the slightest crack necessary to prevent encroachment upon more important interests. It is therefore vital that the standards for judging obscenity safeguard the protection of freedom of speech and press for material which does not treat sex in a manner appealing to prurient interest.

The early leading standard of obscenity allowed material to be judged merely by the effect of an isolated excerpt upon particularly susceptible persons. . . . Some American courts adopted this standard but later decisions have rejected it and substituted this test: whether to the average person, applying contemporary community standards, the dominant theme of the material taken as a whole appeals to prurient interest. The *Hicklin* test, judging obscenity by the effect of isolated passages upon the most susceptible persons, might well encompass material ligitimately treating with sex, and so it must be rejected as unconstitutionally restrictive of the freedoms of speech and press. On the other hand, the substituted standard provides safeguards adequate to withstand the charge of constitutional infirmity.

Both trial courts below sufficiently followed the proper standard. Both courts used the proper definition of obscenity. In addition, in the *Alberts* case, in ruling on a motion to dismiss, the trial judge indicated that, as the trier of facts, he was judging each item as a whole as it would affect the normal person, and in *Roth,* the trial judge instructed the jury as follows:

". . . The test is not whether it would arouse sexual desires or sexual impure thoughts in those comprising a particular segment of the community, the young, the immature or the highly prudish or would leave another segment, the scientific or highly educated or the so-called worldly-wise and sophisticated indifferent and unmoved. . . .

"The test in each case is the effect of the book, picture or publication considered as a whole, not upon any particular class, but upon all those whom it is likely to reach. In other words, you determine its impact upon the average person in the community. The books, pictures and circulars must be judged as a whole, in their entire context, and you are not to consider detached or separate portions in reaching a conclusion. You judge the circulars, pictures and publications which have been put in evidence by present-day standards of the community. You may ask yourselves does it offend the common conscience of the community by present-day standards.

* * *

"In this case, ladies and gentlemen of the jury, you and you alone are the exclusive judges of what the common conscience of the community is, and in determining that conscience you are to consider the community as a whole, young and old, educated and uneducated, the religious and the irreligious—men, women and children."

It is argued that the statutes do not provide reasonably ascertainable standards of guilt and therefore violate the constitutional requirements of due process. . . . The federal obscenity statute makes punishable the mailing of material that is "obscene, lewd, lascivious, or filthy . . . or other publication of an indecent character." The California statute makes punishable, *inter alia,* the keeping for sale or advertising material that is "obscene or indecent." The thrust of the argument is that these words are not sufficiently precise because they do not mean the same thing to all people, all the time, everywhere.

Many decisions have recognized that these terms of obscenity statutes are not precise. This Court, however, has consistently held that lack of precision is not itself offensive to the requirements of due process. ". . . [T]he Constitution does not require impossible standards"; all that is required is that the language "conveys sufficiently definite warning as to the proscribed conduct when measured by common understanding and practices. . . ." These words, applied according to the proper standard for judging obscenity, already discussed, give adequate warning of the conduct proscribed and mark ". . . boundaries sufficiently distinct for judges and juries fairly to administer the law. . . . That there may be marginal cases in which it is difficult to determine the side of the line on which a particular fact situation falls is no sufficient reason to hold the language too ambiguous to define a criminal offense. . . ."

In summary, then, we hold that these statutes, applied according to the proper standard for judging obscenity, do not offend constitutional safeguards against convictions based upon protected material, or fail to give men in acting adequate notice of what is prohibited.

Roth's argument that the federal obscenity statute unconstitutionally encroaches upon the powers reserved by the Ninth and Tenth Amendments to the States and to the people to punish speech and press where offensive to decency and morality is hinged upon his contention that obscenity is expression not excepted from the sweep of the provision of the First Amendment that *"Congress* shall make *no law* . . . abridging the freedom of speech, or of the press. . . ." (Emphasis added.) That argument falls in light of our holding that obscenity is not expression protected by the First Amendment. We therefore hold that the federal obscenity statute punishing the use of the mails for obscene material is a proper exercise of the postal power delegated to Congress by Art. I, § 8, cl. 7. In *United Public Workers v. Mitchell* . . . this Court said:

". . . The powers granted by the Constitution to the Federal Government are subtracted from the totality of sovereignty originally in the states and the people. Therefore, when objection is made that the exercise of a federal power infringes upon rights reserved by the Ninth and Tenth Amendments, the inquiry must be directed toward the granted power under which the action of the Union was taken. If granted power is found, necessarily the objection of invasion of those rights, reserved by the Ninth and Tenth Amendments, must fail. . . ."

Alberts argues that because his was a mail-order business, the California statute is repugnant to Art. I, § 8, cl. 7, under which the Congress allegedly pre-empted the regulatory field by enacting the federal obscenity statute punishing the mailing or advertising by mail of obscene material. The federal statute deals only with actual mailing; it does not eliminate the power of the state to punish "keeping for sale" or "advertising" obscene material. The state statute in no way imposes a burden or interferes with the federal postal functions. ". . . The decided cases which indicate the limits of state regulatory power in relation to the federal mail service involve situations where state regulation involved a direct, physical interference with federal activities under the postal power or some direct, immediate burden on the performance of the postal functions. . . ."

The judgments are *Affirmed.*

> *Justice William O. Douglas, dissenting in both the* Roth *and* Alberts *decisions, warned that under the standards used by the majority, "punishment is inflicted for thoughts provoked, not for overt acts nor antisocial conduct." The "test of obscenity the Court endorses today gives the censor free range over a vast domain." Justice Hugo L. Black concurred in Douglas' dissent, which said:*

. . . When we sustain these convictions, we make the legality of a publication turn on the purity of thought which a book or tract instills in the mind of the reader. I do not think we can approve that standard and be faithful to the command of the First Amendment, which by its terms is a restraint on Congress and which by the Fourteenth is a restraint on the States. . . .

The tests by which these convictions were obtained require only the arousing of sexual thoughts. Yet the arousing of sexual thoughts and desires happens every day in normal life in dozens of ways. Nearly 30 years ago a questionnaire sent to college and normal school women graduates asked what things were most stimulating sexually. Of 409 replies, 9 said "music," 18 said "pictures"; 29 said "dancing"; 40 said "drama"; 95 said "books"; and 218 said "man." . . .

. . . Any test that turns on what is offensive to the community's standards is too loose, too capricious, too destructive of freedom of expression to be squared with the First Amendment. Under that test, juries can censor, suppress, and punish what they don't like, provided the matter relates to "sexual impurity" or has a tendency "to excite lustful thoughts." This is community censorship in one of its worst forms. It creates a regime where in the battle between the literati and the Philistines, the Philistines are certain to win. . . .

. . . Freedom of expression can be suppressed if, and to the extent that, it is so closely brigaded with illegal action as to be an inseparable part of it. . . . As a people, we cannot afford to relax that standard. For the test that suppresses a cheap tract today can suppress a literary gem tomorrow. All it need do is to incite a lascivious thought or arouse a lustful desire. The list of books that judges or juries can place in that category is endless.

I would give the broad sweep of the First Amendment full support. I have the same confidence in the ability of our people to reject noxious literature as I have in their capacity to sort out the true from the false in theology, economics, politics, or any other field.

> *Justice John Marshall Harlan, dissenting in* Roth, *held that "Congress has no substantive power over sexual morality" whereas states "bear direct responsibility for the protection of the local moral fabric." He added:*

. . . I do not think that this conviction can be upheld. The petitioner was convicted under a statute which, under the judge's charge, makes it criminal to sell books which "tend to stir sexual impulses and lead to sexually impure thoughts." I cannot agree that any book which tends to stir sexual impulses and lead to sexually impure thoughts necessarily is "utterly without redeeming social importance." Not only did this charge fail to measure up to the standards which I understand the Court to approve, but as far as I can see, much of the great literature of the world could lead to conviction under such a view of the statute. . . .

Ban on 'Lady Chatterley's Lover' Film Reversed

> *The Supreme Court ruled June 29, 1959 that New York State officials had violated the First and Fourteenth Amendments by refusing a license to exhibit the motion picture "Lady Chatterley's Lover" on the ground that the film was "immoral." Justice Potter Stewart delivered the court's*

opinion (as slightly abridged below) in the case of
Kingsley International Pictures Corp. v. Regents
of the University of the State of New York.

Once again the Court is required to consider the impact of
New York's motion picture licensing law upon First Amendment liberties, protected by the Fourteenth Amendment from infringement by the States. . . .

The New York statute makes it unlawful "to exhibit, or to
sell, lease or lend for exhibition at any place of amusement for
pay or in connection with any business in the state of New York,
any motion picture film or reel [with certain exceptions not relevant here], unless there is at the time in full force and effect a
valid license or permit therefor of the education department. . . ." The law provides that a license shall issue "unless
such film or a part thereof is obscene, indecent, immoral, inhuman, sacrilegious, or is of such a character that its exhibition
would tend to corrupt morals or incite to crime. . . ." A recent
statutory amendment provides that, "the term 'immoral' and the
phrase 'of such a character that its exhibition would tend to corrupt morals' shall denote a motion picture film or part thereof,
the dominant purpose or effect of which is erotic or pornographic; or which portrays acts of sexual immorality, perversion, or
lewdness, or which expressly or impliedly presents such acts as
desirable, acceptable or proper patterns of behavior."

As the distributor of a motion picture entitled "Lady Chatterley's Lover," the appellant Kingsley submitted that film to the
Motion Picture Division of the New York Education Department for a license. Finding three isolated scenes in the film
" 'immoral' within the intent of our Law," the Division refused
to issue a license until the scenes in question were deleted. The
distributor petitioned the Regents of the University of the State
of New York for a review of that ruling. The Regents upheld the
denial of a license, but on the broader ground that "the whole
theme of this motion picture is immoral under said law, for that
theme is the presentation of adultery as a desirable, acceptable
and proper pattern of behavior."

. . . The Appellate Division unanimously annulled the action
of the Regents and directed that a license be issued. . . . A
sharply divided Court of Appeals, however, reversed the Appellate Division and upheld the Regents' refusal to license the film
for exhibition. [*The court's footnote said:* Although four of the

seven judges of the Court of Appeals voted to reverse the order of the Appellate Division, only three of them were of the clear opinion that denial of a license was permissible under the Constitution. Chief Judge Conway wrote an opinion in which Judges Froessel and Burke concurred, concluding that denial of the license was constitutionally permissible. Judge Desmond wrote a separate concurring opinion in which he stated: "I confess doubt as to the validity of such a statute but I do not know how that doubt can be resolved unless we reverse here and let the Supreme Court have the final say."]

The Court of Appeals unanimously and explicitly rejected any notion that the film is obscene. [*The court's footnote said:* The opinion written by Chief Judge Conway stated: "[I]t is curious indeed to say in one breath, as some do, that obscene motion pictures may be censored, and then in another breath that motion pictures which alluringly portray adultery as proper and desirable may not be censored. As stated above, 'The law is concerned with effect, not merely with but one means of producing it.' It must be firmly borne in mind that to give obscenity, as defined, the stature of the only constitutional limitation is to extend an invitation to corrupt the public morals by methods of presentation which craft will insure do not fall squarely within the definition of that term. Precedent, just as sound principle, will not support a statement that motion pictures must be 'out and out' obscene before thay may be censored.". . .]
. . . Rather, the court found that the picture as a whole "alluringly portrays adultery as proper behavior." As Chief Judge Conway's prevailing opinion emphasized, therefore, the only portion of the statute involved in this case is that part of §§ 122 and 122-a of the Education Law requiring the denial of a license to motion pictures "which are immoral in that they *portray* 'acts of sexual immorality . . . as desirable, acceptable or proper patterns of behavior.'" . . . A majority of the Court of Appeals ascribed to that language a precise purpose of the New York Legislature to require the denial of a license to a motion picture "because its subject matter is adultery presented as being right and desirable for certain people under certain circumstances." . . . We accept the premise that the motion picture here in question can be so characterized. We accept too, as we must, the construction of the New York Legislature's language which the Court of Appeals has put upon it. . . . That construction, we emphasize, gives to the term "sexual immorality"

a concept entirely different from the concept embraced in words like "obscenity" or "pornography." Moreover, it is not suggested that the film would itself operate as an incitement to illegal action. Rather, the New York Court of Appeals tells us that the relevant portion of the New York Education Law requires the denial of a license to any motion picture which approvingly portrays an adulterous relationship, quite without reference to the manner of its portrayal.

What New York has done, therefore, is to prevent the exhibition of a motion picture because that picture advocates an idea— that adultery under certain circumstances may be proper behavior. Yet the First Amendment's basic guarantee is of freedom to advocate ideas. The State, quite simply, has thus struck at the very heart of constitutionally protected liberty.

It is contended that the State's action was justified because the motion picture attractively portrays a relationship which is contrary to the moral standards, the religious precepts, and the legal code of its citizenry. This argument misconceives what it is that the Constitution protects. Its guarantee is not confined to the expression of ideas that are conventional or shared by a majority. It protects advocacy of the opinion that adultery may sometimes be proper, no less than advocacy of socialism or the single tax. And in the realm of ideas it protects expression which is eloquent no less than that which is unconvincing.

Advocacy of conduct proscribed by law is not, as Mr. Justice [Louis] Brandeis long ago pointed out, "a justification for denying free speech where the advocacy falls short of incitement and there is nothing to indicate that the advocacy would be immediately acted on." . . . "Among free men, the deterrents ordinarily to be applied to prevent crime are education and punishment for violations of the law, not abridgment of the rights of free speech. . . ." . . . [*The court's footnote said*: Thomas Jefferson wrote more than a hundred and fifty years ago, "But we have nothing to fear from the demoralizing reasonings of some, if others are left free to demonstrate their errors. And especially when the law stands ready to punish the first criminal *act* produced by the false reasoning. These are safer correctives than the conscience of a judge." Letter of Thomas Jefferson to Elijah Boardman, July 3, 1801. . . .]

The inflexible command which the New York Court of Appeals has attributed to the State Legislature thus cuts so close to the core of constitutional freedom as to make it quite needless in this case to examine the periphery. Specifically, there is no occasion to consider the appellant's contention that the State is entirely without power to require films of any kind to be licensed prior to their exhibition. Nor need we here determine whether, despite problems peculiar to motion pictures, the controls which a State may impose upon this medium of expression are precisely coextensive with those allowable for newspapers, books, or individual speech. It is enough for the present case to reaffirm that motion pictures are within the First and Fourteenth Amendments' basic protection. . . . *Reversed*

Justice Hugo L. Black, in a concurring opinion, held that "prior censorship" is unconstitutional. Black wrote:

I concur in the Court's opinion and judgment but add a few words because of concurring opinions by several Justices who rely on their appraisal of the movie *Lady Chatterley's Lover* for holding that New York cannot constitutionally bar it. Unlike them, I have not seen the picture. My view is that stated by Mr. Justice Douglas, that prior censorship of moving pictures like prior censorship of newspapers and books violates the First and Fourteenth Amendments. If despite the Constitution, however, this Nation is to embark on the dangerous road of censorship, my belief is that this Court is about the most inappropriate Supreme Board of Censors that could be found. So far as I know, judges possess no special expertise providing exceptional competency to set standards and to supervise the private morals of the Nation. In addition, the Justices of this Court seem especially unsuited to make the kind of value judgments—as to what movies are good or bad for local communities—which the concurring opinions appear to require. We are told that the only way we can decide whether a State or municipality can constitutionally bar movies is for this Court to view and appraise each movie on a case-by-case basis. Under these circumstances, every member of the Court must exercise his own judgment as to how bad a picture is, a judgment which is ultimately based at least in large part on his own standard of what is immoral. The end result of such decisions seems to me to be a purely personal determination by individual Justices as to whether a particular picture viewed is too bad to allow it to be seen by the public. Such an individualized determination cannot be guided by reasonably fixed and certain standards. Accordingly, neither States nor moving picture makers can possibly know in advance, with any fair degree of certainty, what can or cannot be done in the field of movie making and exhibiting. This uncertainty cannot easily be reconciled with the rule of law which our Constitution envisages. . . .

> *Justice Felix Frankfurter, concurring, held that it was the court's duty to judge, on a case-by-case basis, "whether a particular picture is entitled to the [Fourteenth Amendment's] protection." He wrote:*

As one whose taste in art and literature hardly qualifies him for the *avant-garde*, I am more than surprised, after viewing the picture, that the New York authorities should have banned "Lady Chatterley's Lover." To assume that this motion picture would have offended Victorian moral sensibilities is to rely only on the stuffiest of Victorian conventions. Whatever one's personal preferences may be about such matters, the refusal to license the exhibition of this picture, on the basis of the 1954 amendment to the New York State Educational Law, can only mean that that enactment forbids the public showing of any film that deals with adultery except by way of sermonizing condemnation or depicts any physical manifestation of an illicit amorous relation. Since the denial of a license by the Board of Regents was confirmed by the highest court of the State, I have no choice but to agree with this Court's judgment in holding that the State exceeded the bounds of free expression protected by the "liberty" of the Fourteenth Amendment. But I also believe that the Court's opinion takes ground that exceeds the appropriate limits for decision. . . .

Even the author of "Lady Chatterley's Lover" did not altogether rule out censorship, nor was his passionate zeal on behalf of society's profound interest in the endeavors of true artists so doctrinaire as to be unmindful of the facts of life regarding the sordid exploitation of man's nature and impulses. He knew there was such a thing as pornography, dirt for dirt's sake, or, to be more accurate, dirt for money's sake. This is what D. H. Lawrence wrote:

"But even I would censor genuine pornography, rigorously. It would not be very difficult. In the first place, genuine pornography is almost always underworld, it doesn't come into the open. In the second, you can recognize it by the insult it offers invariably, to sex, and to the human spirit.

"Pornography is the attempt to insult sex, to do dirt on it. This is unpardonable. Take the very lowest instance, the picture postcard sold underhand, by the underworld, in most cities. What I have seen of them have been of an ugliness to make you cry. The insult to the human body, the insult to a vital human relationship! Ugly and cheap they make the human nudity, ugly and degraded they make the sexual act, trivial and cheap and nasty." (D. H. Lawrence, Pornography and Obscenity, pp. 12-13.)

This traffic has not lessened since Lawrence wrote. Apparently it is on the increase. In the course of the recent debate in both Houses of Parliament on the Obscene Publications Bill, . . . designed to free British authors from the hazards of too rigorous application in our day of Lord Cockburn's ruling, in 1868, in *Regina* v. *Hicklin*, . . . weighty experience was adduced regarding the extensive dissemination of pornographic materials. . . . Nor is there any reason to believe that on this side of the ocean there has been a diminution in the pornographic business which years ago sought a flourishing market in some of the leading secondary schools for boys, who presumably had more means than boys in the public high schools.

It is not surprising, therefore, that the pertinacious, eloquent and free-spirited promoters of the liberalizing legislation in Great Britain did not conceive the needs of a civilized society, in assuring the utmost freedom to those who make literature and art possible—authors, artists, publishers, producers, book sellers–easily attainable by sounding abstract and unqualified dogmas about freedom. They had a keen awareness that freedom of expression is no more an absolute than any other freedom. . . .

In short, there is an evil against which a State may constitutionally protect itself, whatever we may think about questions of policy involved. The real problem is the formulation of constitutionally allowable safeguards which society may take against evil without impinging upon the necessary dependence of a free society upon the fullest scope of free expression. . . .

. . . Ours is the vital but very limited task of scrutinizing the work of the [legislative] draftsmen in order to determine whether they have kept within the narrow limits of the kind of censorship which even D. H. Lawrence deemed necessary. The legislation must not be so vague, the language so loose, as to leave to those who have to apply it too wide a discretion for sweeping within its condemnation what is permissible expression as well as what society may permissibly prohibit. Always remembering that the widest scope of freedom is to be given to the adventurous and imaginative exercise of the human spirit, we have struck down legislation phrased in language intrinsically vague, unless it be responsive to the common understanding of men even though not susceptible of explicit definition. The ultimate reason for invalidating such laws is that they lead to timidity and inertia and thereby discourage the boldness of expression indispensable for a progressive society.

The New York legislation of 1954 was the product of careful lawyers who sought to meet decisions of this Court which had left no doubt that a motion-picture licensing law is not inherently outside the scope of the regulatory powers of a State under the Fourteenth Amendment. The Court does not strike the law down because of vagueness, as we struck down prior New York legislation. Nor does it reverse the judgment of the New York Court of Appeals, as I would, because in applying the New York law to "Lady Chatterley's Lover" it applied it to a picture to which it cannot be applied without invading the area of constitutionally free expression. The difficulty which the Court finds seems to derive from some expressions culled here and there from the opinion of the Chief Judge of the New York Court of Appeals. This leads the Court to give the phrase "acts of sexual immorality . . as desirable, acceptable or proper patterns of behavior" an innocent content, meaning, in effect, an allowable subject matter for discussion. But surely, to attribute that result to the decision of the Court of Appeals, on the basis of a few detached phrases of Chief Judge Conway, . . . is to forget that the meaning of language is to be felt and its phrases not to be treated disjointedly. "Sexual immorality" is not a new phrase in this branch of law and its implications dominate the context. I hardly conceive it possible that the Court would strike down as unconstitutional the federal statute against mailing lewd, obscene and lascivious matter, which has been the law of the land for nearly a hundred years. . . . In sustaining this legislation this Court gave the words "lewd, obscene and lascivious" concreteness by saying that they concern "sexual immorality." . . .

Unless I misread the opinion of the Court, it strikes down the

New York legislation in order to escape the task of deciding whether a particular picture is entitled to the protection of expression under the Fourteenth Amendment. Such an exercise of the judicial function, however onerous or ungrateful, inheres in the very nature of the judicial enforcement of the Due Process Clause. We cannot escape such instance-by-instance, case-by-case application of that clause in all the varieties of situations that come before this Court. . . .

> *Justice William O. Douglas, joined by Justice Hugo L. Black, concurred in the decision but did so on the basis of his view that film censorship violated the constitutional guarantees. Douglas wrote:*

While I join in the opinion of the Court, I adhere to the vews I expressed in *Superior Films* v. *Department of Education* . . . that censorship of movies is unconstitutional, since it is a form of "previous restraint" that is as much at war with the First Amendment, made applicable to the States through the Fourteenth, as the censorship struck down in *Near* v. *Minnesota.* . . . If a particular movie violates a valid law, the exhibitor can be prosecuted in the usual way. I can find in the First Amendment no room for any censor whether he is scanning an editorial, reading a news broadcast, editing a novel or a play, or previewing a movie.

Reference is made to British law and British practice. But they have little relevance to our problem, since we live under a written Constitution. What is entrusted to the keeping of the legislature in England is protected from legislative interference or regulation here. As we stated in *Bridges* v. *California*, . . . "No purpose in ratifying the Bill of Rights was clearer than that of securing for the people of the United States much greater freedom of religion, expression, assembly, and petition than the people of Great Britain had ever enjoyed." If we had a provision in our Constitution for "reasonable" regulation of the press such as India has included in hers, there would be room for argument that censorship in the interests of morality would be permissible. Judges sometimes try to read the word "reasonable" into the First Amendment or make the rights it grants subject to reasonable regulation . . . or apply to the States a watered-down version of the First Amendment. But its language, in terms that are absolute, is utterly at war with censorship. Different questions may arise as to censorship of some news when the Nation is actually at war. But any possible exceptions are extremely limited. . . .

Happily government censorship has put down few roots in this country. The American tradition is represented by *Near* v. *Minnesota, supra*. . . . We have in the United States no counterpart of the Lord Chamberlain who is censor over England's stage. As late as 1941 only six States had systems of censorship for movies. . . . That number has now been reduced to four— Kansas, Maryland, New York, and Virginia—plus a few cities. Even in these areas, censorship of movies shown on television gives way by reason of the Federal Communications Act. . . . And from what information is available, movie censors do not seem to be very active. Deletion of the residual part of censorship that remains would constitute the elimination of an institution that intrudes on First Amendment rights.

> *Justice Tom Clark, concurring in the decision, based his opinion on what he indicates was a flaw in the New York statute in that "it placed more emphasis on [the confusing issue of] what the film teaches than on what it depicts." Clark wrote:*

I can take the words of the majority of the New York Court of Appeals only in their clear, unsophisticated and common meaning. They say that §§ 122 and 122-a of New York's Education Law "require the denial of a license to motion pictures which are immoral in that they portray 'acts of sexual immorality . . . as desirable, acceptable or proper patterns of behavior.' " That court states the issue in the case in this language: "Moving pictures are our only concern and, what is more to the point, only those motion pictures which alluringly present acts of sexual immorality as proper behavior." . . . Moreover, it is significant to note that in its 14-page opinion that court says again and again . . . that the picture "Lady Chatterley's Lover" is proscribed because of its "espousal" of sexual immorality as "desirable" or as "proper conduct for the people of our State."

The minority of my brothers here, however, twist this holding into one that New York's Act requires "obscenity or incitement, not just abstract expressions of opinion." But I cannot so obliterate the repeated declarations above-mentioned that were made not only 15 times by the Court of Appeals but which were the basis of the Board of Regents' decision as well. Such a construction would raise many problems, not the least of which would be our failure to accept New York's interpretation of the scope of its own Act. I feel . . . bound by their holding.

In this context, the Act comes within the ban of *Joseph Burstyn, Inc.*, v. *Wilson*, . . . (1952). We held there that "expression by means of motion pictures is included within the free speech and free press guaranty of the First and Fourteenth Amendments." . . . Referring to *Near* v. *Minnesota* . . . (1931), we said that while "a major purpose of the First Amendment guaranty of a free press was to prevent prior restraints upon publication" such protection was not unlimited but did place on the State "a heavy burden to demonstrate that the limitation challenged" was exceptional. . . . The standard applied there was the word "sacrilegious" and we found it set the censor "adrift upon a boundless sea amid a myriad of conflicting currents of religious views. . . ." . . . We struck it down.

Here the standard is the portrayal of "acts of sexual immorality . . . as desirable, acceptable or proper patterns of behavior." Motion picture plays invariably have a hero, a villain, supporting characters, a location, a plot, a diversion from the main theme and usually a moral. As we said in *Burstyn*: "They may affect public attitudes and behavior in a variety of ways, ranging from direct espousal of a political or social doctrine to the subtle shaping of thought which characterizes all artistic expression."

. . . What may be to one viewer the glorification of an idea as being "desirable, acceptable or proper" may to the notions of another be entirely devoid of such a teaching. The only limits on the censor's discretion is his understanding of what is included within the term "desirable, acceptable or proper." This is nothing less than a roving commission in which individual impressions become the yardstick of action, and result in regulation in accordance with the beliefs of the individual censor rather than regulation by law. Even here three of my brothers "cannot regard this film as depicting anything more than a somewhat unusual, and rather pathetic, 'love triangle.'" At least three—perhaps four—of the members of New York's highest court thought otherwise. I need only say that the obscurity of the standard presents such a choice of difficulties that even the most experienced find themselves at dagger's point.

It may be, as Chief Judge Conway said, "that our public morality, possibly more than ever before, needs every protection government can give." . . . And, as my Brother Harlan points out, "each time such a statute is struck down, the State is left in more confusion." This is true where broad grounds are employed leaving no indication as to what may be necessary to meet the requirements of due process. I see no grounds for confusion, however, were a statute to ban "pornographic" films, or those that "portray *acts* of sexual immorality, perversion or lewdness." If New York's statute had been so construed by its highest court I believe it would have met the requirements of due process. Instead, it placed more emphasis on what the film teaches than on what it depicts. There is where the confusion enters. For this reason, I would reverse on the authority of *Burstyn*.

> *Justice John Marshall Harlan concurred in the decision to reverse the conviction but did so on the ground that in the application to the film of the provisions of the New York statute, "constitutional bounds were exceeded." He rejected the majority's opinion that these provisions "are unconstitutional on their face." In an opinion in which Justices Felix Frankfurter and Charles Evans Whittaker joined, Harlan wrote:*

I think the Court has moved too swiftly in striking down a statute which is the product of a deliberate and conscientious effort on the part of New York to meet constitutional objections raised by this Court's decisions respecting predecessor statutes in this field. . . .

Section 122-a of the State Education Law was passed in 1954 to meet this Court's decision in *Commercial Pictures Corp.* v. *Regents*, . . . which overturned the New York Court of Appeals' holding in *In re Commercial Pictures Corp.* v. *Board of Regents* . . . that the film *La Ronde* could be banned as "immoral" and as "tend[ing] to corrupt morals" under § 122. [A footnote points out that Section 122 provides: "The director of the [motion picture] division or, when authorized by the regents, the officers of a local office or bureau shall cause to be promptly examined every motion picture film submitted to them as herein required, and unless such film or a part thereof is obscene, indecent, immoral, inhuman, sacrilegious, or is of such a character that its exhibition would tend to corrupt morals or incite to crime, shall issue a license thereof. If such director or, when so authorized, such officer shall not license any film submitted, he shall furnish to the applicant therefor a written report of the reasons for his refusal and a description of each rejected part of a film not rejected in toto."] The Court's decision in *Commercial Pictures* was but a one line *per curiam* with a citation to *Joseph Burstyn, Inc.* v. *Wilson*, . . . which in turn had held for naught not the word "immoral" but the term "sacrilegious" in the statute.

New York, nevertheless, set about repairing its statute. This it did by enacting § 122-a which in the respects emphasized in the present opinion of Chief Judge Conway as pertinent here defines an "immoral" motion picture film as one which portrays " 'acts of sexual immorality . . . as desirable, acceptable or proper patterns of behavior.' " . . . [A footnote reports that Section 122-a provides: "1. For the purpose of section one hundred twenty-two of this chapter, the term 'immoral' and the phrase 'of such a character that its exhibition would tend to corrupt morals' shall denote a motion picture film or part thereof, the dominant purpose or effect of which is erotic or pornographic; or which portrays acts of sexual immorality, perversion, or lewdness, or which expressly or impliedly presents such acts as desirable, acceptable or proper patterns of behavior. 2. For the purpose of section one hundred twenty-two of this chapter, the term 'incite to crime' shall denote a motion picture the dominant purpose or effect of which is to suggest that the commission of criminal acts or contempt for law is profitable, desirable, acceptable, or respectable behavior; or which advocates or teaches the use of, or the methods of use of, narcotics or habit-forming drugs."] The Court now holds this part of New York's effort unconstitutional on its face under the Fourteenth Amendment. I cannot agree.

The Court does not suggest that these provisions are bad for vagueness. [According to a footnote, the bill that became § 122-a was introduced at the request of the State Education Department, which noted . . . that "the issue of censorship, as such, is not involved in this bill. This bill merely attempts to follow out the criticism of the United States Supreme Court by defining the words 'immoral' and 'incite to crime.' " . . . In a memorandum accompanying his approval of the measure, the then Governor of New York, himself a lawyer, wrote: "Since 1921, the Education Law of this State has required the licensing of motion pictures and authorized refusal of a license for a motion picture which is 'obscene, indecent, immoral' or which would 'tend to corrupt morals or incite to crime.' Recent Supreme Court decisions have indicated that the term 'immoral' may not be sufficiently definite for constitutional purposes. The primary purpose of this bill is to define 'immoral' and 'tend to corrupt morals' in conformance with the apparent requirements of these cases. It does so by defining them in terms of 'sexual immorality.' The words selected for this definition are based on judicial opinions which have given exhaustive and reasoned treatment to the subject. The bill does not create any new licensing system, expand the scope of motion picture censorship, or enlarge the area of permissible prior restraint. Its sole purpose is to give to the section more precision to make it conform to the tenor of recent court decisions and proscribe the exploitation of 'filth for the sake of filth.' It does so as accurately as language permits in 'words well understood through long use.' . . . The language of the Supreme Court of the United States, in a recent opinion of this precise problem, should be noted: To hold that liberty and expression by means of motion pictures is guaranteed by the First and Fourteenth Amendments, however, is not the end of the problem. It does not follow that the Constitution requires absolute freedom to exhibit every motion picture of every kind at all times and all places.' (*Burstyn* v. *Wilson* . . .) So long as the State has the responsibility for interdicting motion pictures which transgress the bounds of decency, we have the responsibility for furnishing guide lines to the agency charged with enforcing the law." . . .] Any such suggestion appears to me untenable in view of the long-standing usage in this Court of the concept "sexual immorality" to explain in part the meaning of "obscenity." . . . [A footnote adds: Certainly it cannot be claimed that adultery is not a form of "sexual immorality"; indeed adultery is made a crime in New York . . .] Instead, the Court finds a constitutional vice in these provisions in that they require, so it is said, neither "obscenity" not incitement to "sexual immorality," but strike of their own force at the mere advocacy of "an idea—that adultry under certain circumstances may be proper behavior"; expressions of "opinion that adultery may sometimes be proper. . . ." I think this characterization of these provisions misconceives the construction put upon them by the prevailing opinions in the Court of Appeals. Granting that the abstract public discussion or advocacy of adultery, unac-

companied by obscure portrayal or actual incitement to such behavior, may not constitutionally be proscribed by the State, I do
not read those opinions to hold that the statute on its face undertakes any such proscription. Chief Judge Conway's opinion,
which was joined by two others of the seven judges of the Court
of Appeals, and in the thrust of which one more concurred, to be
sure with some doubt, states . . . : "It should first be emphasized that the scope of section 122-a is not mere expression of
opinion in the form, for example, of a filmed lecture whose subject matter is the espousal of adultery. We reiterate that this
case involves the espousal of sexually immoral acts (here adultry) *plus* actual scenes of a suggestive and obscene nature." (Emphasis in the original.)

The opinion elsewhere, as indeed is also the case with §§ 122
and 122-a themselves when independently read in their entirety,
is instinct with the notion that mere abstract expressions of opinion regarding the desirability of sexual immorality, unaccompanied by obscenity or incitement, are not proscribed. . . . It
is the corruption of public morals, occasioned by the inciting
effect of a particular portrayal or by what New York has deemed
the necessary effect of obscenity, at which the statute is aimed.
In the words of Chief Judge Conway, "There is no difference in
substance between motion pictures which are corruptive of the
public morals, and sexually suggestive, because of a predomi-
nance of suggestive scenes, and those which achieve precisely
the same effect by presenting only several such scenes in a clearly approbatory manner throughout the course of the film. *The
law is concerned with effect, not merely with but one means of
producing it . . . the objection lies in the corrosive effect upon
the public sense of sexual morality.*" . . . (Emphasis in original.) . . .

'Lady Chatterley's Lover' Held Not Obscene

> *In a ruling issued in U.S. District Court in New
> York July 21, 1959, Federal Judge Frederick Van
> Pelt Bryan relied in large part on the* Ulysses *and*
> Roth *decisions in holding that D. H. Lawrence's
> novel* Lady Chatterley's Lover, *in an unexpurgat-
> ed edition, was not obscene. Bryan delivered this
> decision (slightly abridged) in the case of* Grove
> Press, Inc. and Readers' Subscription, Inc. v.

Robert K. Christenberry, individually and as
Postmaster of the City of New York:

These two actions against the Postmaster of New York arise
out of the denial of the United States mails to the recently published Grove Press unexpurgated edition of "Lady Chatterley's
Lover" by D. H. Lawrence.

Plaintiffs seek to restrain the Postmaster from enforcing a decision of the Post Office Department that the unexpurgated
"Lady Chatterley's Lover," and circulars announcing its availability, are non-mailable under the statute barring obscene matter
from the mails. . . . They also seek a declaratory judgment to
the effect (1) that the novel is not "obscene, lewd, lascivious,
indecent or filthy" in content or character, and is not non-mailable under the statute or, in the alternative, (2) that if the novel be
held to fall within the purview of the statute, the statute is to that
extent invalid and violates plaintiffs' rights in contravention of
the First and Fifth Amendments.

Grove Press, Inc., one of the plaintiffs, is the publisher of the
book. Readers' Subscription, Inc., the other plaintiff, is a book
club which has rights to distribute it.

[1] . . . On April 30, 1959 the New York Postmaster withheld
from dispatch some 20,000 copies of circulars deposited for
mailing by Readers' Subscription, which announced the availability of the new Grove edition of *Lady Chatterley*. At about the
same time he also detained a number of copies of the book
which had been deposited for mailing by Grove Press.

[2] On May 8, 1959 letters of complaint issued by the General
Counsel of the Post Office Department were served on Grove
and Readers' Subscription alleging that there was probable
cause to believe that these mailings violated 18 U.S.C. § 1461,
and advising them of a departmental hearing. The respondents
filed answers denying these allegations and a hearing was held
before the Judicial Officer of the Post Office Department on
May 14, 1959.

The General Counsel, as complainant, introduced the Grove
edition and the circulars which had been detained and rested.

The respondents offered (1) testimony as to their reputation
and standing in the book publishing and distribution fields and
their purpose in publishing and distributing the novel; (2) reviews of the book in leading newspapers and literary periodicals
throughout the country; (3) copies of editorials and comments in

leading newspapers concerning publication of the book and its anticipated impact; (4) news articles dealing with the banning of the book by the Post Office; and (5) expert testimony by two leading literary critics, Malcolm Cowley and Alfred Kazin, as to the literary stature of the work and its author; contemporary acceptance of literature dealing with sex and sex relations and their own opinions as to the effect of the book on its readers. The editorials and comments and the news articles were excluded.

The Judicial Officer before whom the hearing was held did not decide the issues. On May 28 he issued an order referring the proceedings to the Postmaster General "for final departmental decision."

On June 11, 1959 the Postmaster General rendered a departmental decision finding that the Grove edition "is obscene and non-mailable pursuant to 18 U.S. Code § 1461," and that the Readers' Subscription circulars "give information where obscene material, namely, the book in issue in this case, may be obtained and are non-mailable. . . ."

I

The basic question here is whether the unexpurgated "Lady Chatterley's Lover" is obscene within the meaning of 18 U.S.C. § 1461, and is thus excluded from the protections afforded freedom of speech and the press by the First Amendment.

However, the defendant takes the position that this question is not before me for decision. He urges that the determination by the Postmaster General that this novel is obscene and non-mailable is conclusive upon the court unless it is found to be unsupported by substantial evidence and is clearly wrong. He argues, therefore, that I may not determine the issue of obscenity *de novo*.

Thus, an initial question is raised as to the scope of the court's power of review. In the light of the issues presented, the basis of the Postmaster General's decision, and the record before him, this question is not of substance.

(1) Prior to *Roth v. United States* . . . the Supreme Court had "always assumed that obscenity is not protected by the freedoms of speech and press." However, until then the constitutional question had not been directly passed upon by the court. In *Roth* the question was squarely posed.

The court held, in accord with its long-standing assumption, that "obscenity is not within the area of constitutionally protected speech or press."

The court was faced with a dilemma. On the one hand it was required to eschew any impingement upon the cherished freedoms of speech and the press guaranteed by the Constitution and so essential to a free society. On the other hand it was faced with the recognized social evil presented by the purveyance of pornography.

The opinion of Mr. Justice Brennan for the majority makes it plain that the area which can be excluded from constitutional protection without impinging upon the free speech and free press guarantees is narrowly limited. He says . . . :

"All ideas having even the slightest redeeming social importance—unorthodox ideas, controversial ideas, even ideas hateful to the prevailing climate of opinion—have the full protection of the guarantees, unless excludable because they encroach upon the limited area of more important interests."

He gives stern warning that no publication advancing such ideas can be suppressed under the guise of regulation of public morals or censorship of public reading matter. . . .

It was against the background of these constitutional requirements that the Court laid down general standards for judging obscenity, recognizing that it was "vital that [such] standards . . . safeguard the protection of freedom of speech and press for material which does not treat sex" in an obscene manner. The standards were "whether to the average person, applying contemporary community standards, the dominant theme of the material taken as a whole appeals to prurient interest." . . .

Plainly application of these standards to specific material may involve no little difficulty as the court was well aware. Cases involving "hard core" pornography, or what Judge Woolsey referred to as "dirt for dirt's sake," purveyed furtively by dealers in smut, are relatively simple. But works of literary merit present quite a different problem, and one which the majority in *Roth* did not reach as such.

Chief Justice [Earl] Warren, concurring in the result, said of this problem . . . :

". . . The history of the application of laws designed to suppress the obscene demonstrates convincingly that the power of government can be invoked under them against great art or literature, scientific treatises, or works exciting social controversy.

Mistakes of the past prove that there is a strong countervailing interest to be considered in the freedoms guaranteed by the First and Fourteenth Amendments."

And Mr. Justice Harlan, dissenting, also deeply concerned, had this to say . . . :

". . . The suppression of a particular writing or other tangible form of expression is . . . an *individual* matter, and in the nature of things every such suppression raises an individual constitutional problem, in which a reviewing court must determine for *itself* whether the attacked expression is suppressible within constitutional standards. Since those standards do not readily lend themselves to generalized definitions, the constitutional problem in the last analysis becomes one of particularized judgments which appellate courts must make for themselves.

"I do not think that reviewing courts can escape this responsibility by saying that the trier of the facts, be it a jury or a judge, has labeled the questioned matter as 'obscene,' for, if 'obscenity' is to be suppressed, the question whether a particular work is of that character involves not really an issue of fact but a question of constitutional *judgment* of the most sensitive and delicate kind."

Mr. Justice Frankfurter, concurring in *Kingsley International Pictures Corp. v. Regents,* . . . expressed a similar view. He pointed out that in determining whether particular works are entitled to the constitutional protections of freedom of expression "We cannot escape such instance-by-instance, case-by-case . . . [constitutional adjudication] in all the variety of situations that come before this Court." And Mr. Justice Harlan, in the same case, also concurring in the result, speaks of "the necessity for individualized adjudication. In the very nature of things the problems in this area are ones of individual cases. . . ."

It would seem that the Court itself made such "individualized" or "case by case" adjudications as to the obscenity of specific material in at least two cases following *Roth.* In *One, Inc. v. Olesen* . . . and *Sunshine Book Co. v. Summerfield* . . . the courts below had found in no uncertain terms that the material was obscene within the meaning of Section 1461. In each case the Supreme Court in a one sentence per curiam opinion granted certiorari and reversed on the authority of *Roth.*

One, Inc. v. Olesen, and *Sunshine Book Co. v. Summerfield,* involved determination by the Post Office barring material from the mails on the ground that it was obscene. In both the District Court had found that the publication was obscene and that the determination of the Post Office should be upheld. In both the Court of Appeals had affirmed the findings of the District Court.

Yet in each the Supreme Court, without discussion, summarily reversed on the authority of *Roth*. As Judge Desmond of the New York Court of Appeals said of these cases—"Presumably, the court having looked at those books simply held them not to be obscene."

[3] It is no less the duty of this court in the case at bar to scrutinize the book with great care and to determine for itself whether it is within the constitutional protections afforded by the First Amendment, or whether it may be excluded from those protections because it is obscene under the *Roth* tests.

(2) Such review is quite consistent with the Administrative Procedure Act, assuming that the act is applicable here. . . .

The complainant relied on the text of the novel and nothing more to establish obscenity. Respondents' evidence was wholly uncontradicted, and, except for the opinions of the critics Cowley and Kazin as to the effect of the book upon its readers, it scarcely could have been. The complainant conceded that the book had literary merit. The views of the critics as to the place of the novel and its author in twentieth century English literature have not been questioned.

As the Postmaster General said, he attempted to apply to the book "the tests which, it is my understanding, the courts have established for determining questions of obscenity." Thus, all he did was to apply the statute, as he interpreted it in the light of the decisions, to the book. His interpretation and application of the statute involved questions of law, not questions of fact.

The Postmaster General has no special competence or technical knowledge on this subject which qualifies him to render an informed judgment entitled to special weight in the courts. . . . [H]e has no special competence to determine what constitutes obscenity within the meaning of Section 1461, or that "contemporary community standards are not such that this book should be allowed to be transmitted in the mails" or that the literary merit of the book is outweighed by its pornographic features, as he found. Such questions involve interpretation of a statute, which also imposes criminal penalties, and its application to the allegedly offending material. The determination of such questions is peculiarly for the courts, particularly in the light of the constitutional questions implicit in each case. . . .

[4] Assuming power in the Postmaster General to withhold obscene matter from dispatch in the mails temporarily, a grant of discretion to make a final determination as to whether a book is obscene and should be denied to the public should certainly not be inferred in the absence of a clear and direct mandate. As the Supreme Court pointed out under comparable circumstances in *Hannegan v. Esquire, Inc.,* . . . to vest such power in the Postmaster General would, in effect, give him the power of censorship and that "is so abhorrent to our traditions that a purpose to grant it should not be easily inferred."

[5] No such grant of power to the Postmaster General has been called to my attention and I have found none. Whatever administrative functions the Postmaster General has go no further than closing the mails to material which is obscene within the meaning of the statute. This is not an area in which the Postmaster General has any "discretion" which is entitled to be given special weight by the courts.

The Administrative Procedure Act makes the reviewing court responsible for determining all relevant questions of law, for interpreting and applying all constitutional and statutory provisions and for setting aside agency action not in accordance with law. . . . The question presented here falls within this framework.

Thus, the question presented for decision is whether "Lady Chatterley's Lover" is obscene within the meaning of the statute and thus excludable from constitutional protections. . . .

II

This unexpurgated edition of "Lady Chatterley's Lover" has never before been published either in the United States or England, though comparatively small editions were published by Lawrence himself in Italy and authorized for publication in France, and a number of pirated copies found their way to this country.

Grove Press is a reputable publisher with a good list which includes a number of distinguished writers and serious works. Before publishing this edition Grove consulted recognized literary critics and authorities on English literature as to the advisability of publication. All were of the view that the work was of major literary importance and should be made available to the American public.

No one is naive enough to think that Grove Press did not expect to profit from the book. Nevertheless the format and composition of the volume, the advertising and promotional material and the whole approach to publication, treat the book as a serious work of literature. The book is distributed through leading bookstores throughout the country. There has been no attempt by the publisher to appeal to prurience or the prurient minded.

The Grove edition has a preface by Archibald MacLeish, former Librarian of Congress, Pulitzer Prize winner, and one of this country's most distinguished poets and literary figures, giving his appraisal of the novel. There follows an introduction by Mark Schorer, Professor of English Literature at the University of California, a leading scholar of D. H. Lawrence and his work. The introduction is a critique of the novel against the background of Lawrence's life, work and philosophy. At the end of the novel there is a bibliographical note as to the circumstances under which it was written and first published. Thus, the novel is placed in a setting which emphasizes its literary qualities and its place as a significant work of a major English novelist.

Readers' Subscription has handled the book in the same vein. The relatively small number of Readers' Subscription subscribers is composed largely of people in academic, literary and scholarly fields. Its list of books includes works of high literary merit, including books by and about D. H. Lawrence.

There is nothing of "the leer of the sensualist" in the promotion or methods of distribution of this book. There is no suggestion of any attempt to pander to the lewd and lascivious minded for profit. The facts are all to the contrary.

Publication met with unanimous critical approval. The book was favorably received by the literary critics of such diverse publications as the *New York Times,* the *Chicago Tribune,* the *San Francisco Call Bulletin,* the *New York Post,* the *New York Herald Tribune, Harpers* and *Time,* to mention only some. The critics were not agreed upon their appraisal. Critical comment ranged from acclaim on the one hand to more restrained views that this was not the best of Lawrence's writing, and was dated and in parts "wooden." But as MacLeish says in the preface,

". . . in spite of these reservations no responsible critic would deny the book a place as one of the most important works of fiction of the century, and no reader of any kind could undertake to express an opinion about the literature of the time or about the spiritual history that literature expresses without making his peace in one way or another with D. H. Lawrence and with this work.''

Publication of the Grove edition was a major literary event. It was greeted by editorials in leading newspapers throughout the country unanimously approving the publication and viewing with alarm possible attempts to ban the book.

It was against this background that the New York Postmaster impounded the book and the Postmaster General barred it. The decision of the Postmaster General, in a brief of four pages, relied on three cases, *Roth v. United States, supra; United States v. One Book Called "Ulysses,"* . . . and *Besig v. United States.* . . . While he quotes from *Roth* the Postmaster General relies principally on *Besig,* which was not reviewed by the Supreme Court. It may be noted that the Ninth Circuit relied heavily on *Besig* in *One Book, Inc. v. Olesen, supra,* which was summarily reversed by the Supreme Court on the authority of *Roth.*

He refers to the book as ''currently withheld from the mails in the United States and barred from the mails by several other major nations.'' His only discussion of its content is as follows:

''The contemporary community standards are not such that this book should be allowed to be transmitted in the mails.

''The book is replete with descriptions in minute detail of sexual acts engaged in or discussed by the book's principal characters. These descriptions utilize filthy, offensive and degrading words and terms. Any literary merit the book may have is far outweighed by the pornographic and smutty passages and words, so that the book, taken as a whole, is an obscene and filthy work.

''I therefore see no need to modify or reverse the prior rulings of this Department and the Department of the Treasury with respect to this edition of this book.''

This seems to be the first time since the notable opinions of Judge Woolsey and Judge Augustus Hand in *United States v. One Book Called "Ulysses," supra,* in 1934 that a book of comparable literary stature has come before the federal courts charged with violating the federal obscenity statutes. . . .

[6] The essence of the Ulysses holdings is that a work of literary merit is not obscene under federal law merely because it contains passages and language dealing with sex in a most candid and realistic fashion and uses many four-letter Anglo-Saxon

words. Where a book is written with honesty and seriousness of purpose, and the portions which might be considered obscene are relevant to the theme, it is not condemned by the statute even though "it justly may offend many." "Ulysses" contains numerous passages dealing very frankly with sex and the sex act and is free in its use of four-letter Anglo-Saxon words. Yet both Judge Woolsey in the District Court, and Judge Hand in the Court of Appeals, found that it was a sincere and honest book which was not in any sense "dirt for dirt's sake." They both concluded that "Ulysses" was a work of high literary merit, written by a gifted and serious writer, which did not have the dominant effect of promoting lust or prurience and therefore did not fall within the interdiction of the statute.

Roth v. United States, supra, decided by the Supreme Court in 1957, twenty-three years later, unlike the *Ulysses* case, did not deal with the application of the obscenity statutes to specific material. It laid down general tests circumscribing the area in which matter is excludable from constitutional protections because it is obscene, so as to avoid impingement on First Amendment guarantees.

The court distilled from the prior cases (including the *Ulysses* case, which it cited with approval) the standards to be applied—"whether to the average person, applying contemporary community standards, the dominant theme of the material taken as a whole appeals to prurient interest."

The court saw no significant difference between this expression of the standards and those in the American Law Institute Model Penal Code to the effect that

". . . A thing is obscene if, considered as a whole, its predominant appeal is to prurient interest, i.e., a shameful or morbid interest in nudity, sex, or excretion, and if it goes substantially beyond customary limits of candor in description or representation of such matters. . . ."

These standards are not materially different from those applied in *Ulysses* to the literary work considered there. Since the *Roth* case dealt with these standards for judging obscenity in general terms and the *Ulysses* case dealt with application of such standards to a work of recognized literary stature, the two should be read together.

A number of factors are involved in the application of these tests.

As Mr. Justice Brennan pointed out in *Roth,* sex and obscenity are by no means synonymous and "[t]he portrayal of sex, *e. g.,* in art, literature and scientific works, is not in itself sufficient reason to deny material the constitutional protection of freedom of speech and press." As he said, sex has been "a subject of absorbing interest to mankind through the ages; it is one of the vital problems of human interest and public concern." The subject may be discussed publicly and truthfully without previous restraint or fear of subsequent punishment as long as it does not fall within the narrowly circumscribed interdicted area.

[7] Both cases held that, to be obscene, the dominant effect of the book must be an appeal to prurient interest—that is to say, shameful or morbid interest in sex. Such a theme must so predominate as to submerge any ideas of "redeeming social importance" which the publication contains.

[8] It is not the effect upon the irresponsible, the immature or the sensually minded which is controlling. The material must be judged in terms of its effect on those it is likely to reach who are conceived of as the average man of normal sensual impulses. . . .

[9, 10] The material must also exceed the limits of tolerance imposed by current standards of the community with respect to freedom of expression in matters concerning sex and sex relations. Moreover, a book is not to be judged by excerpts or individual passages but must be judged as a whole.

All of these factors must be present before a book can be held obscene and thus outside constitutional protections.

Judged by these standards, "Lady Chatterley's Lover" is not obscene. The decision of the Postmaster General that it is obscene and therefore non-mailable is contrary to law and clearly erroneous. This is emphasized when the book is considered against its background and in the light of its stature as a significant work of a distinguished English novelist.

D. H. Lawrence is one of the most important novelists writing in the English language in this century. . . .

The text of this edition of "Lady Chatterley's Lover" was written by Lawrence toward the close of his life and was his third version of the novel, originally called "Tenderness."

The book is almost as much a polemic as a novel.

In it Lawrence was expressing his deep and bitter dissatisfaction with what he believed were the stultifying effects of advancing industrialization and his own somewhat obscure philosophic remedy of a return to "naturalness." He attacks what he considered to be the evil effects of industrialization upon the wholesome and natural life of all classes in England. In his view this was having disastrous consequences on English society and on the English countryside. It had resulted in devitalization of the upper classes of society and debasement of the lower classes. One result, as he saw it, was the corrosion of both the emotional and physical sides of man as expressed in his sexual relationships which had become increasingly artificial and unwholesome.

The novel develops the contrasts and conflicts in characters under these influences.

The plot is relatively simple.

Constance Chatterley is married to a baronet, returned from the first world war paralyzed from the waist down. She is physically frustrated and dissatisfied with the artificiality and sterility of her life and of the society in which she moves. . . . Failing to find satisfaction in an affair with a man in her husband's circle, Constance Chatterley finds herself increasingly restless and unhappy. Her husband half-heartedly urges her to have a child by another man whom he will treat as his heir. Repelled by the suggestion that she casually beget a child, she is drawn to Mellors, the gamekeeper, sprung from the working class who, having achieved a measure of spiritual and intellectual independence, is a prototype of Lawrence's natural man. They establish a deeply passionate and tender relationship which is described at length and in detail. At the conclusion she is pregnant and plans to obtain a divorce and marry the gamekeeper.

This plot serves as a vehicle through which Lawrence develops his basic theme of contrast between his own philosophy and the sterile and debased society which he attacks. Most of the characters are prototypes. The plot and theme are meticulously worked out with honesty and sincerity.

The book is replete with fine writing and with descriptive passages of rare beauty. There is no doubt of its literary merit.

It contains a number of passages describing sexual intercourse in great detail with complete candor and realism. Four-letter Anglo-Saxon words are used with some frequency.

These passages and this language understandably will shock the sensitive minded. Be that as it may, these passages are relevant to the plot and to the development of the characters and of their lives as Lawrence unfolds them. The language which shocks, except in a rare instance or two, is not inconsistent with character, situation or theme.

Even if it be assumed that these passages and this language taken in isolation tend to arouse shameful, morbid and lustful sexual desires in the average reader, they are an integral, and to the author a necessary part of the development of theme, plot and character. The dominant theme, purpose and effect of the book as a whole is not an appeal to prurience or the prurient minded. The book is not "dirt for dirt's sake." Nor do these passages and this language submerge the dominant theme so as to make the book obscene even if they could be considered and found to be obscene in isolation.

What the Postmaster General seems to have done is precisely what the Supreme Court in *Roth* and the courts in the *Ulysses* case said ought not to be done. He has lifted from the novel individual passages and language, found them to be obscene in isolation and therefore condemned the book as a whole. He has disregarded the dominant theme and effect of the book and has read these passages and this language as if they were separable and could be taken out of context. Thus he has "weighed" the isolated passages which he considered obscene against the remainder of the book and concluded that the work as a whole must be condemned.

[11] Writing about sex is not in itself pornographic, as the Postmaster General recognized. Nor does the fact that sex is a major theme of a book condemn the book as obscene. Neither does the use of "four letter" words, despite the offense they may give. "Ulysses" was found not to be obscene despite long passages containing similar descriptions and language. . . .

[12] The tests of obscenity are not whether the book or passages from it are in bad taste or shock or offend the sensibilities of an individual, or even of a substantial segment of the community. Nor are we concerned with whether the community would approve of Constance Chatterley's morals. The statute does not purport to regulate the morals portrayed or the ideas expressed in a novel, whether or not they are contrary to the accepted moral code, nor could it constitutionally do so. . . .

Plainly "Lady Chatterley's Lover" is offensive to the Postmaster General. . . . I do not personally find the book offensive.

But the personal views of neither of us are controlling here. The standards for determining what constitutes obscenity under this statute have been laid down. These standards must be objectively applied regardless of personal predilections.

There has been much discussion of the intent and purpose of Lawrence in writing *Lady Chatterley*. It is suggested that the intent and purpose of the author has no relevance to the question as to whether his work is obscene and must be disregarded.

[13] No doubt an author may write a clearly obscene book in the mistaken belief that he is serving a high moral purpose. The fact that this is the author's purpose does not redeem the book from obscenity.

But the sincerity and honesty of purpose of an author as expressed in the manner in which a book is written and in which his theme and ideas are developed has a great deal to do with whether it is of literary and intellectual merit. Here, as in the *Ulysses* case, there is no question about Lawrence's honesty and sincerity of purpose, artistic integrity and lack of intention to appeal to prurient interest.

Thus, this is an honest and sincere novel of literary merit and its dominant theme and effect, taken as a whole, is not an appeal to the prurient interest of the average reader.

This would seem to end the matter. However, the Postmaster General's finding that the book is non-mailable because it offends contemporary community standards bears some discussion.

I am unable to ascertain upon what the Postmaster General based this conclusion. The record before him indicates general acceptance of the book throughout the country and nothing was shown to the contrary. The critics were unanimous. Editorial comment by leading journals of opinion welcomed the publication and decried any attempts to ban it.

[14] It is true that the editorial comment was excluded by the Judicial Officer at the hearing. But it seems to me that this was error. These expressions were relevant and material on the question of whether the book exceeded the limits of freedom of expression in matters involving sex and sex relations tolerated by the community at large in these times.

The contemporary standards of the community and the limits of its tolerance cannot be measured or ascertained accurately. There is no poll available to determine such questions. Surely expressions by leading newspapers, with circulations of millions, are some evidence at least as to what the limits of tolerance by present day community standards are, if we must embark upon a journey of exploration into such uncharted territory.

Quite apart from this, the broadening of freedom of expression and of the frankness with which sex and sex relations are dealt with at the present time require no discussion. In one best selling novel after another frank descriptions of the sex act and "four-letter" words appear with frequency. These trends appear in all media of public expression, in the kind of language used and the subjects discussed in polite society, in pictures, advertisements and dress, and in other ways familiar to all. Much of what is now accepted would have shocked the community to the core a generation ago. Today such things are generally tolerated whether we approve or not.

[15, 16] I hold that, at this stage in the development of our society, this major English novel, does not exceed the outer limits of the tolerance which the community as a whole gives to writing about sex and sex relations.

One final word about the constitutional problem implicit here.

It is essential to the maintenance of a free society that the severest restrictions be placed upon restraints which may tend to prevent the dissemination of ideas. It matters not whether such ideas be expressed in political pamphlets or works of political, economic or social theory or criticism, or through artistic media. All such expressions must be freely available.

A work of literature published and distributed through normal channels by a reputable publisher stands on quite a different footing from hard core pornography furtively sold for the purpose of profiting by the titillation of the dirty minded. The courts have been deeply and properly concerned about the use of obscenity statutes to suppress great works of art or literature. As Judge Augustus Hand said in *Ulysses* . . . :

". . . The foolish judgments of Lord Eldon about one hundred years ago, proscribing the works of Byron and Southey, and the finding by the jury under a charge by Lord Denman that the publication of Shelley's 'Queen Mab' was an indictable offense are a warning to all who have to determine the limits of the field within which authors may exercise themselves."

To exclude this book from the mails on the grounds of obscenity would fashion a rule which could be applied to a substantial portion of the classics of our literature. Such a rule would be inimical to a free society. To interpret the obscenity statute so as to bar "Lady Chatterley's Lover" from the mails would render the statute unconstitutional in its application, in violation of the guarantees of freedom of speech and the press contained in the First Amendment.

It may be, as the plaintiffs urge, that if a work is found to be of literary stature, and not "hard core" pornography, it is *a fortiori* within the protections of the First Amendment. But I do not reach that question here. For I find that "Lady Chatterley's Lover" is not obscene within the meaning of 18 U.S.C. § 1461, and is entitled to the protections guaranteed to freedoms of speech and press by the First Amendment. I therefore hold that the order of the Postmaster General is illegal and void and violates plaintiffs' rights in contravention of the Constitution. . . .

Jacobellis Ruling Expands Roth Freedoms

> *In a split decision that expanded the* Roth *ruling's requirements for findings of obscenity, the Supreme Court June 22, 1964 reversed the conviction of an Ohio film theater manager who had been convicted of possessing and showing an obscene film. Justice William J. Brennan, announcing the decision of the court but delivering an opinion in which only Justice Arthur Goldberg joined, held that a work could be proscribed only if it were "utterly" without social importance and if it substantially exceeded "customary limits of candor in description or representation." Brennan also held that the "contemporary community standards" test referred to national not local standards. In the case of* Jacobellis v. Ohio, *Brennan wrote:*

Appellant, Nico Jacobellis, manager of a motion picture theatre in Cleveland Heights, Ohio, was convicted on two counts of possessing and exhibiting an obscene film in violation of Ohio Revised Code (1963 Supp.), § 2905.34. [Footnote: "*Selling, exhibiting, and possessing obscene literature or drugs, for criminal purposes.* No person shall knowingly sell, lend, give away, exhibit, or offer to sell, lend, give away, or exhibit, or publish or offer to publish or have in his possession or under his control an obscene, lewd, or lascivious book, magazine, pamphlet, paper, writing, advertisement, circular, print, picture, photograph, motion picture film, or book, pamphlet, paper, mag-

azine not wholly obscene but containing lewd or lascivious articles, advertisements, photographs, or drawing, representation,
figure, image, cast, instrument, or article of an indecent or immoral nature, or a drug, medicine, article, or thing intended for
the prevention of conception or for causing an abortion, or advertise any of them for sale, or write, print, or cause to be written or printed a card, book, pamphlet, advertisement, or notice
giving information when, where, how, of whom, or by what
means any of such articles or things can be purchased or obtained, or manufacture, draw, print, or make such articles or
things, or sell, give away, or show to a minor, a book, pamphlet,
magazine, newspaper, story paper, or other paper devoted to the
publication, or principally made up, of criminal news, police reports, or accounts of criminal deeds, or pictures and stories of
immoral deeds, lust, or crime, or exhibit upon a street or high-
way or in a place which may be within the view of a minor, any
of such books, papers, magazines, or pictures. . . .] . . . His
conviction, by a court of three judges . . . , was affirmed by an
intermediate appellate court . . . and by the Supreme Court of
Ohio . . . The dispositive question is whether the state courts
properly found that the motion picture involved, a French film
called *"Les Amants"* ("The Lovers"), was obscene and hence
not entitled to the protection for free expression that is guaranteed by the First and Fourteenth Amendments. We conclude
that the film is not obscene and that the judgement must accordingly be reversed.

Motion pictures are within the ambit of the constitutional
guarantees of freedom of speech and of the press. *Joseph Burstyn, Inc.,* v. *Wilson.* . . . But in *Roth* v. *United States* and *Alberts* v. *California* . . . we held that obscenity is not subject to
those guarantees. Application of an obscenity law to suppress a
motion picture thus requires ascertainment of the "dim and uncertain line" that often separates obscenity from constitutionally protected expression. . . . It has been suggested that this is
a task in which our Court need not involve itself. . . . Since it
is only "obscenity" that is excluded from the constitutional protection, the question whether a particular work is obscene necessarily implicates an issue of constitutional law. . . . Such an
issue, we think, must ultimately be decided by this Court. Our
duty admits of no substitute for facing up to the tough individual
problems of constitutional judgment involved in every obscenity
case." . . .

In other areas involving constitutional rights under the Due Process Clause, the Court has consistently recognized its duty to apply the applicable rules of law upon the basis of an independent review of the facts of each case. . . . And this has been particularly true where rights have been asserted under the First Amendment guarantees of free expression. Thus in *Pennekamp* v. *Florida*, . . . the Court stated: "The Constitution has imposed upon this Court final authority to determine the meaning and application of those words of that instrument which require interpretation to resolve judicial issues. With that responsibility, we are compelled to examine for ourselves the statements in issue and the circumstances under which they were made to see whether or not they . . . are of a character which the principles of the First Amendment, as adopted by the Due Process Clause of the Fourteenth Amendment, protect." We cannot understand why the Court's duty should be any different in the present case, where Jacobellis has been subjected to a criminal conviction for disseminating a work of expression and is challenging that conviction as a deprivation of rights guaranteed by the First and Fourteenth Amendments. Nor can we understand why the Court's performance of its constitutional and judicial function in this sort of case should be denigrated by such epithets as "censor" or "super-censor." In judging alleged obscenity the Court is no more "censoring" expression than it has in other cases "censored" criticism of judges and public officials, advocacy of governmental overthrow, or speech alleged to constitute a breach of the peace. Use of an opprobrious label can neither obscure nor impugn the Court's performance of its obligation to test challenged judgements against the guarantees of the First and Fourteenth Amendments and, in doing so, to delineate the scope of constitutionally protected speech. Hence we reaffirm the principle that, in "obscenity" cases as in all others involving rights derived from the First Amendment guarantees of free expression, this Court cannot avoid making an independent constitutional judgement on the facts of the case as to whether the material involved is constitutionally protected.

The question of the proper standard for making this determination has been the subject of much discussion and controversy since our decision in *Roth* seven years ago. Recognizing that the test for obscenity enunciated there—"whether to the average person, applying contemporary community standards, the dominant theme of the material taken as a whole appeals to prurient interest," . . . —is not perfect, we think any substitute would raise equally difficult problems, and we therefore adhere to that standard. We would reiterate, however, our recognition in *Roth* that obscenity is excluded from the constitutional protection only because it is "utterly without redeeming social importance," and that "the portrayal of sex, *e. g.*, in art, literature and scientific works, is not itself sufficient reason to deny material the constitutional protection of freedom of speech and press." . . . It follows that material dealing with sex in a manner that advocates ideas, . . . or that has literary or scientific or artistic value or any other form of social importance, may not be branded as obscenity and denied the constitutional protection. Nor may the constitutional status of the material be made to turn on a "weighing" of its social importance against its prurient appeal, for a work cannot be proscribed unless it is "utterly" without social importance. . . . It should also be recognized that the *Roth* standard requires in the first instance a finding that the material "goes substantially beyond customary limits of candor in description or representation of such matters." This was a requirement of the Model Penal Code test that we approved in *Roth*, . . . and it is explicitly reaffirmed in the more recent Proposed Official Draft of the Code. [The footnote provides this definition of the American Law Institute, Model Penal Code, Proposed Official Draft (May 4, 1962), § 251.4 (1): "Material is obscene if, considered as a whole, its predominant appeal is to prurient interest . . . and if *in addition* it goes substantially beyond customary limits of candor in describing or representing such matters." (Italics added.)] In the absence of such a deviation from society's standards of decency, we do not see how any official inquiry into the allegedly prurient appeal of a work of expression can be squared with the guarantees of the First and Fourteenth Amendments. . . .

It has been suggested that the "contemporary community standards" aspect of the *Roth* test implies a determination of the constitutional question of obscenity in each case by the standards of the particular local community from which the case arises. This is an incorrect reading of *Roth*. The concept of "contemporary community standards" was first expressed by Judge Learned Hand in *United States* v. *Kennerley* . . . (1913), where he said: "Yet, if the time is not yet when men think innocent all that which is honestly germane to a pure subject, however little it may mince its words, still I scarcely think that they would forbid all which might corrupt the most corruptible, or that society is prepared to accept for its own limitations those which may perhaps be necessary to the weakest of its members. If there be no abstract definition, such as I have suggested, should not the word 'obscene' be allowed to indicate the present critical point in the compromise between candor and shame at which *the community may have arrived here and now?* . . . To put thought in leash to the *average conscience of the time* is perhaps tolerable, but to fetter it by the necessities of the lowest and least capable seems a fatal policy. Nor is it an objection, I think, that such an interpretation gives to the words of the statute a varying meaning from time to time. Such words as these do not embalm the precise morals of an age or place; while they presuppose that some things will always be shocking to the public taste, the vague subject-matter is left to the gradual development of general notions about what is decent. . . . '' (Italics added.) It seems clear that in this passage Judge Hand was referring not to state and local "communities,'' but rather to "the community" in the sense of "society at large; . . . the public, or people in general.'' Thus, he recognized that under his standard the concept of obscenity would have "a varying meaning from time to time"—not from county to county, or town to town.

We do not see how any "local" definition of the "community" could properly be employed in delineating the area of expression that is protected by the Federal Constitution. Mr. Justice Harlan pointed out in *Manual Enterprises, Inc.,* v. *Day* . . . that a standard based on a particular local community would have "the intolerable consequence of denying some sections of the country access to material, there deemed acceptable, which in others might be considered offensive to prevailing community standards of decency. Cf. *Butler* v. *Michigan.* . . . '' . . . It can hardly be assumed that all the patrons of a particular library, bookstand, or motion picture theatre are residents of the smallest local "community" that can be drawn around that establishment. Furthermore, to sustain the suppression of a particular book or film in one locality would deter its dissemination in other localities where it might be held not obscene, since sellers and exhibitors would be reluctant to risk criminal conviction in testing the variation between the two places. It would be a hardy person who would sell a book or exhibit a film anywhere in the land after this Court had sustained the judgement of one "community" holding it to be outside the constitutional protection. The result would thus be "to restrict the public's access to forms of the printed word which the State could not constitutionally suppress directly." *Smith* v. *California. . . .*

. . . The Court has explicitly refused to tolerate a result whereby "the constitutional limits of free expression in the Nation would vary with state lines," *Pennekamp* v. *Florida . . .* ; we see even less justification for allowing such limits to vary with town or county lines. We thus reaffirm the position taken in *Roth* to the effect that the constitutional status of an allegedly obscene work must be determined on the basis of a national standard. . . .

We recognize the legitimate and indeed exigent interest of States and localities throughout the Nation in preventing the dissemination of material deemed harmful to children. But that interest does not justify a total suppression of such material, the effect of which would be to "reduce the adult population . . . to reading only what is fit for children." *Butler* v. *Michigan. . . .* Since the present conviction is based upon exhibition of the film to the public at large and not upon its exhibition to children, the judgment must be reviewed under the strict standard applicable in determining the scope of the expression that is protected by the Constitution.

We have applied that standard to the motion picture in question. "The Lovers" involves a woman bored with her life and marriage who abandons her husband and family for a young archaeologist with whom she has suddenly fallen in love. There is an explicit love scene in the last reel of the film, and the State's objections are based almost entirely upon that scene. The film was favorably reviewed in a number of national publications, although disparaged in others, and was rated by at least two critics of national stature among the best films of the year in which it was produced. It was shown in approximately 100 of the larger cities in the United States, including Columbus and Toledo, Ohio. We have viewed the film, in the light of the record made in the trial court, and we conclude that it is not obscene within the standards enunciated in *Roth* v. *United States* and *Alberts* v. *California*, which we reaffirm here.   *Reversed.*

> *Chief Justice Earl Warren, joined by Justice Tom Clark, dissented, citing the* Roth *decision. He wrote:*

In this and other cases in this area of the law, which are coming to us in ever-increasing numbers, we are faced with the resolution of rights basic both to individuals and to society as a whole. Specifically, we are called upon to reconcile the right of the Nation and of the States to maintain a decent society and, on the other hand, the right of the individuals to express themselves freely in accordance with the guarantees of the First and Fourteenth Amendments. Although the Federal Government and virtually every State has had laws proscribing obscenity since the Union was formed, and although this Court has recently decided that obscenity is not within the protection of the First Amendment, neither courts nor legislatures have been able to evolve a truly satisfactory definition of obscenity. . . . The obscenity problem . . . is aggravated by the fact that it involves the area of public expression, an area in which a broad range of freedom is vital to our society and is constitutionally protected.

Recently this Court put its hand to the task of defining the term "obscenity" in *Roth* v. *United States*. . . . The definition enunciated in that case has generated much legal speculation as well as further judicial interpretation by state and federal courts. It has also been relied upon by legislatures. Yet obscenity cases continue to come to this Court, and it becomes increasingly apparent that we must settle as well as we can the question of what constitutes "obscenity" and the question of what standards are permissible in enforcing proscriptions against obscene matter. This Court hears cases such as the instant one not merely to rule upon the alleged obscenity of a specific film or book but to establish principles for the guidance of lower courts and legislatures. Yet most of our decisions since *Roth* have been given without opinion and have thus failed to furnish such guidance. Nor does the Court in the instant case—which has now been twice argued before us—shed any greater light on the problem. Therefore, I consider it appropriate to state my views at this time.

For all the sound and fury that the *Roth* test has generated, it has not been proved unsound, and I believe that we should try to live with it—at least until a more satisfactory definition is evolved. No government—be it federal, state, or local—should be forced to choose between repressing all material, including that within the realm of decency, and allowing unrestrained license to publish any material, no matter how vile. There must be a rule of reason in this as in other areas of the law, and we have attempted in the *Roth* case to provide such a rule.

It is my belief that when the Court said in *Roth* that obscenity is to be defined by reference to "community standards," it meant community standards—not a national standard, as is sometimes argued. I believe that there is no provable "national standard," and perhaps there should be none. At all events, this Court has not been able to enunciate one, and it would be unreasonable to expect local courts to divine one. It is said that such a "community" approach may well result in material being proscribed as obscene in one community but not in another, and, in all probability, that is true. But communities throughout the Nation are in fact diverse, and it must be remembered that, in cases such as this one, the Court is confronted with the task of reconciling conflicting rights and the diverse communities within our society and of individuals.

We are told that only "hard core pornography" should be denied the protection of the First Amendment. But who can define "hard core pornography" with any greater clarity than "obscenity"? And even if we were to retreat to that position we would soon be faced with the need to define that term just as we now are faced with the need to define "obscenity." Meanwhile, those who profit from the commercial exploitation of obscenity would continue to ply their trade unmolested.

In my opinion, the use to which various materials are put—not just the words and pictures themselves—must be considered in determining whether or not the materials are obscene. A technical or legal treatise on pornography may well be inoffensive under most circumstances but, at the same time, "obscene" in the extreme when sold or displayed to children. [Footnote: In the instant case, for example, the advertisements published to induce the public to view the motion picture provide some evidence of the film's dominant theme: "When all conventions explode . . . in the most daring love story ever filmed!" "As close to authentic amour as is possible on the screen." "The frankest love scenes yet seen on film." "Contains one of the longest and most sensuous love scenes to be seen in this country."]

Finally, material which is in fact obscene under the *Roth* test may be proscribed in a number of ways—for instance, by confiscation of the material or by prosecution of those who disseminate it—provided always that the proscription, whatever it may be, is imposed in accordance with constitutional standards. . . .

In light of the foregoing, I would reiterate my acceptance of the rule of the *Roth* case: Material is obscene and not constitutionally protected against regulation and proscription if "to the average person, applying contemporary community standards, the dominant theme of the material taken as a whole appeals to prurient interest." . . . I would commit the enforcement of this rule to the appropriate state and federal courts, and I would accept their judgements made pursuant to the *Roth* rule, limiting myself to a consideration only of whether there is sufficient evidence in the record upon which a finding of obscenity could be made. If there is no evidence in the record upon which such a finding could be made, obviously the material involved cannot be held obscene. . . . But since a mere modicum of evidence may satisfy a "no evidence" standard, I am unwilling to give the important constitutional right of free expression such limited protection. However, protection of society's right to maintain its moral fiber and the effective administration of justice require that this Court not establish itself as an ultimate censor, in each case reading the entire record, viewing the accused material, and making an independent *de novo* judgment on the question of obscenity. Therefore, once a finding of obscenity has been made below under a proper application of the *Roth* test, I would apply a "sufficient evidence" standard of review—requiring something more than merely any evidence but something less than "substantial evidence on the record [including the allegedly obscene material] as a whole." . . . This is the only reasonable way I can see to obviate the necessity of this Court's sitting as the Super Censor of all the obscenity purveyed throughout the Nation.

While in this case, I do not subscribe to some of the State's extravagant contentions, neither can I say that the courts below acted with intemperance or without sufficient evidence in finding the moving picture obscene within the meaning of the *Roth* test. Therefore, I would affirm the judgment.

'Fanny Hill' Obscenity Judgment Reversed

> *The Supreme Court March 21, 1966 reversed the findings of the Massachusetts state courts that John Cleland's 200-year-old novel generally known as* Fanny Hill *was obscene and therefore not entitled to the protection of the First and*

Fourteenth Amendments. Justice William J. Brennan, in an opinion in which Chief Justice Earl Warren and Justice Abe Fortas joined, asserted that each of three elements must be satisfied independently before a book can be held obscene: (a) the dominant theme of the material taken as a whole appeals to a prurient interest in sex; (b) the material is patently offensive because it affronts contemporary community standards on sex matters, and (c) the material is utterly without redeeming social value. Announcing the court's decision, Brennan wrote:

This is an obscenity case in which *Memoirs of a Woman of Pleasure* (commonly known as *Fanny Hill*, written by John Cleland in about 1750, was adjudged obscene in a proceeding that put on trial the book itself, and not its publisher or distributor. The proceeding was a civil equity suit brought by the Attorney General of Massachusetts, pursuant to General Laws of Massachusetts, Chapter 272, §§ 28C-28H, to have the book declared obscene. . . .

[A footnote included this summary of the testimony of experts in the Massachusetts proceedings:

["In the view of one or another or all of the following viz., the chairman of the English department at Williams College, a professor of English at Harvard College, an associate professor of English literature at Boston University, an associate professor of English at Massachusetts Institute of Technology, and an assistant professor of English and American literature at Brandeis University, the book is a minor 'work of art' having 'literary merit' and 'historical value' and containing a good deal of deliberate, calculated comedy.' It is a piece of 'social history of interest to anyone who is interested in fiction as a way of understanding society in the past.' A saving grace is that although many scenes, if translated into the present day language of 'the realistic, naturalistic novel, could be quite offensive' these scenes are not described in such language. The book contains no dirty words and its language 'functions . . . to create a distance, even when the sexual experiences are portrayed.' The response, therefore, is a literary response. The descriptions of depravity are not obscene because 'they are subordinate to an interest which is primarily literary'; Fanny's reaction to the scenes of depravity was 'anger,' 'disgust, horror, [and] indignation.' The book 'belongs to the history of English literature rather than the history of smut.' "

["One of the witnesses testified in part as follows: 'Cleland is part of what I should call this cultural battle that is going on in the 18th century, a battle between a restricted Puritan, moralistic ethic that attempts to suppress freedom of the spirit, freedom of the flesh, and this element is competing with a freer attitude towards life, a more generous attitude towards life, a more wholesome attitude towards life, and this very attitude that is manifested in Fielding's great novel "Tom Jones" is also evident in Cleland's novel. . . . [Richardson's] "Pamela" is the story of a young country girl; [his] "Clarissa" is the story of a woman trapped in a house of prostitution. Obviously, then Cleland takes both these themes, the country girl, her initiation into life and into experience, and the story of a woman in a house of prostitution, and what he simply does is to take the situation and reverse the moral standards. Richardson believed that chastity was the most important thing in the world; Cleland and Fielding obviously did not and thought there were more important significant moral values.' "

["In the opinion of the other academic witness, the headmaster of a private school, whose field is English literature, the book is without literary merit and is obscene, impure, hard core pornography, and is patently offensive."]

. . . The trial justice entered a final decree, which adjudged *Memoirs* obscene and declared that the book "is not entitled to the protection of the First and Fourteenth Amendments to the Constitution of the United States against action by the Attorney General or other law enforcement officer pursuant to the provisions of . . . § 28B, or otherwise." The Massachusetts Supreme Judicial Court affirmed the decree. . . . *We reverse.*

[Section 28B made it a criminal offense, *inter alia*, to import, print, publish, sell, loan, distribute, buy, procure, receive, or possess for the purpose of sale, loan, or distribution, "a book, knowing it to be obscene."]

I.

The term "obscene" appearing in the Massachusetts statute has been interpreted by the Supreme Judicial Court to be as expansive as the Constitution permits: the "statute covers all material that is obscene in the constitutional sense." . . . Thus the sole question before the state courts was whether *Memoirs* satisfies the test of obscenity established in *Roth v. United States* . . . .

We defined obscenity in *Roth* in the following terms: "[W]hether to the average person, applying contemporary community standards, the dominant theme of the material taken as a whole appeals to prurient interest." . . . Under this definition, as elaborated in subsequent cases, three elements must coalesce: it must be established that (a) the dominant theme of the material taken as a whole appeals to a prurient interest in sex; (b) the material is patently offensive because it affronts contemporary community standards relating to the description or representation of sexual matters; and (c) the material is utterly without redeeming social value.

The Supreme Judicial Court purported to apply the *Roth* definition of obscenity and held all three criteria satisfied. We need not consider the claim that the court erred in concluding that *Memoirs* satisfied the prurient appeal and patent offensiveness criteria; for reversal is required because the court misinterpreted the social value criterion. The court applied the criterion in this passage: "It remains to consider whether the book can be said to be 'utterly without social importance.' We are mindful that there was expert testimony . . . to the effect that *Memoirs* is a structural novel with literary merit; that the book displays a skill in characterization and a gift for comedy; that it plays a part in the history of the development of the English novel; and that it contains a moral, namely, that sex with love is superior to sex in a brothel. But the fact that the testimony may indicate this book has some minimal literary value does not mean it is of any social importance. We do not interpret the 'social importance' test as requiring that a book which appeals to prurient interest and is patently offensive must be unqualifiedly worthless before it can be deemed obscene." . . .

The Supreme Judicial Court erred in holding that a book need not be "unqualifiedly worthless before it can be deemed obscene." A book cannot be proscribed unless it is found to be *utterly* without redeeming social value. This is so even though the book is found to possess the requisite prurient appeal and to be patently offensive. Each of the three federal constitutional criteria is to be applied independently; the social value of the book can neither be weighed against nor canceled by its prurient appeal or patent offensiveness. [A footnote quoted from the California decision in the case of *Zeitlin v. Arnebergh* (1963): "[M]aterial dealing with sex in a manner that advocates ideas . . . or that has literary or scientific or artistic value or any other form of social importance, may not be branded as obscenity and denied the constitutional protection. Nor may the constitutional status of the material be made to turn on a 'weighing' of its social importance against its prurient appeal, for a work cannot be proscribed unless it is 'utterly' without social importance . . ."] Hence, even on the view of the court below that *Memoirs* possessed only a modicum of social value, its judgment must be reversed as being founded on an erroneous interpretation of a federal constitutional standard.

II.

It does not necessarily follow from this reversal that a determination that *Memoirs* is obscene in the constitutional sense would be improper under all circumstances. On the premise, which we have no occasion to assess, that *Memoirs* has the requisite prurient appeal and is patently offensive, but has only a minimum of social value, the circumstances of production, sale, and publicity are relevant in determining whether or not the publication or distribution of the book is constitutionally protected. Evidence that the book was commercially exploited for the sake of prurient appeal, to the exclusion of all other values, might justify the conclusion that the book was utterly without redeeming social importance. It is not that in such a setting the social value test is relaxed so as to dispense with the requirement that a book be *utterly* devoid of social value, but rather that, as we elaborate in *Ginzburg v. United States, post*, pp. 470-473, where the purveyor's sole emphasis is on the sexually provocative aspects of his publications, a court could accept his evaluation at its face value. In this proceeding, however, the courts were asked to judge the obscenity of *Memoirs* in the abstract, and the declaration of obscenity was neither aided nor limited by a specific set of circumstances of production, sale, and publicity. All possible uses of the book must therefore be considered, and the mere risk that the book might be exploited by panderers because it so pervasively treats sexual matters cannot alter the fact—given the view of the Massachusetts court attributing to *Memoirs* a modicum of literary and historical value—that the book will have redeeming social importance in the hands of those who publish or distribute it on the basis of that value.   *Reversed.*

Justice William O. Douglas, concurring in the judgment, reiterated his contention that Fanny Hill *could not be proscribed since the First Amendment forbids censorship of ideas not linked with legal action. He rejected the view expressed in* Roth *that "obscene" speech is "outside" the protection of the First Amendment. Douglas wrote:*

Memoirs of a Woman of Pleasure, or, as it is often titled, *Fanny Hill,* concededly is an erotic novel. It was first published in about 1749 and has endured to this date, despite periodic efforts to suppress it. [A footnote said: *Memoirs* was the subject of what is generally regarded as the first recorded suppression of a literary work in this country on grounds of obscenity. . . . The edition there condemned differed from the present volume in that it contained apparently erotic illustrations.] The book relates the adventures of a young girl who becomes a prostitute in London. At the end, she abandons that life and marries her first lover, observing:

"Thus, at length, I got snug into port, where, in the bosom of virtue, I gather'd the only uncorrupt sweets: where, looking back on the course of vice I had run, and comparing its infamous blandishments with the infinitely superior joys of innocence, I could not help pitying even in point of taste, those who, immers'd in gross sensuality, are insensible to the so delicate charms of VIRTUE, than which even PLEASURE has not a greater friend, nor than VICE a greater enemy. Thus temperance makes men lords over those pleasures that intemperance enslaves them to: the one, parent of health, vigour, fertility, cheerfulness, and every other desirable good of life; the other, of diseases, debility, barrenness, self-loathing, with only every evil incident to human nature.

". . . The paths of Vice are sometimes strew'd with roses, but then they are for ever infamous for many a thorn, for many a cankerworm: those of Virtue are strew'd with roses purely, and those eternally unfading ones."

In 1963, an American publishing house undertook the publication of *Memoirs.* The record indicates that an unusually large number of orders were placed by universities and libraries; the Library of Congress requested the right to translate the book into Braille. But the Commonwealth of Massachusetts instituted the suit that ultimately found its way here, praying that the book be declared obscene so that the citizens of Massachusetts might be spared the necessity of determining for themselves whether or not to read it.

The courts of Massachusetts found the book "obscene" and upheld its suppression. This Court reverses, the prevailing opinion having seized upon language in the opinion of the Massachusetts Supreme Judicial Court in which it is candidly admitted that *Fanny Hill* has at least "some minimal literary value." I do not believe that the Court should decide this case on so disingenuous a basis as this. I base my vote to reverse on my view that the First Amendment does not permit the censorship of expression not brigaded with illegal action. But even applying the prevailing view of the *Roth* test, reversal is compelled by this record which makes clear that *Fanny Hill* is not "obscene." The prosecution made virtually no effort to prove that this book is "utterly without redeeming social importance." The defense, on the other hand, introduced considerable and impressive testimony to the effect that this was a work of literary, historical, and social importance.

We are judges, not literary experts or historians or philosophers. We are not competent to render an independent judgment as to the worth of this or any other book, except in our capacity as private citizens. . . . If there is to be censorship, the wisdom of experts on such matters as literary merit and historical significance must be evaluated. On this record, the Court has no choice but to reverse the judgment of the Massachusetts Supreme Judicial Court, irrespective of whether we would include *Fanny Hill* in our own libraries.

Four of the seven Justices of the Massachusetts Supreme Judicial Court conclude that *Fanny Hill* is obscene. . . . Four of the seven judges of the New York Court of Appeals conclude that it is not obscene. . . . To outlaw the book on such a voting record would be to let majorities rule where minorities were thought to be supreme. The Constitution forbids abridgment of "freedom of speech, or of the press." Censorship is the most notorious form of abridgment. It substitutes majority rule where minority tastes or viewpoints were to be tolerated.

It is to me inexplicable how a book that concededly has social worth can nonetheless be banned because of the manner in which it is advertised and sold. However florid its cover, whatever the pitch of its advertisements, the contents remain the same.

Every time an obscenity case is to be argued here, my office is flooded with letters and postal cards urging me to protect the community or the Nation by striking down the publication. The messages are often identical even down to commas and semicolons. The inference is irresistible that they were all copied from a school or church blackboard. Dozens of postal cards often are mailed from the same precinct. The drives are incessant and the pressures are great. Happily we do not bow to them. I mentioned them only to emphasize the lack of popular understanding of our constitutional system. Publications and utterances were made immune from majoritarian control by the First Amendment, applicable to the States by reason of the Fourteenth. No exceptions were made, not even for obscenity. The Court's contrary conclusion in *Roth*, where obscenity was found to be "outside" the First Amendment, is without justification.

The extent to which the publication of "obscenity" was a crime at common law is unclear. It is generally agreed that the first reported case involving obscene conduct is *The King* v. *Sir Charles Sedley* [a 1663 action]. Publication of obscene literature, at first thought to be the exclusive concern of the ecclesiastical courts, was not held to constitute an indictable offense until 1727. A later case involved the publication of an "obscene and impious libel" (a bawdy parody of Pope's "Essay on Man") by a member of the House of Commons [in 1770]. On the basis of these few cases, one cannot say that the common-law doctrines with regard to publication of obscenity were anything but uncertain. "There is no definition of the term. There is no basis of identification. There is no unity in describing what is obscene literature, or in prosecuting it. There is little more than the ability to smell it." Alpert, Judicial Censorship of Obscene Literature, 52 Harv. L. Rev. 40, 47 (1938).

But even if the common law had been more fully developed at the time of the adoption of the First Amendment, we would not be justified in assuming that the Amendment left the common law unscathed. In *Bridges* v. *California*, . . . we said: "[T]o assume that English common law in this field became ours is to deny the generally accepted historical belief that 'one of the objects of the Revolution was to get rid of the English common law on liberty of speech and of the press.' Schofield, *Freedom of the Press in the United States*, 9 Publications Amer. Sociol. Soc., 67, 76.

"More specifically, it is to forget the environment in which the First Amendment was ratified. In presenting the proposals which were later embodied in the Bill of Rights, James Madison, the leader in the preparation of the First Amendment, said: 'Although I know whenever the great rights, the trial by jury, freedom of the press, or liberty of conscience, come in question in that body [Parliament], the invasion of them is resisted by able advocates, yet their Magna Charta does not contain any one provision for the security of those rights, respecting which the people of America are most alarmed. The freedom of the press and rights of conscience, those choicest privileges of the people, are unguarded in the British Constitution.'" . . .

It is true, as the Court observed in *Roth*, that obscenity laws appeared on the books of a handful of States at the time the First Amendment was adopted. But the First Amendment was, until the adoption of the Fourteenth, a restraint only upon federal power. Moreover, there is an absence of any *federal* cases or laws relative to obscenity in the period immediately after the adoption of the First Amendment. Congress passed no legislation relating to obscenity until the middle of the nineteenth century. Neither reason nor history warrants exclusion of any particular class of expression from the protection of the First Amendment on nothing more than a judgment that it is utterly without merit. . . .

The censor is always quick to justify his function in terms that are protective of society. But the First Amendment, written in terms that are absolute, deprives the States of any power to pass on the value, the propriety, or the morality of a particular expression. . . .

Perhaps the most frequently assigned justification for censorship is the belief that erotica produce antisocial sexual conduct. But that relationship has yet to be proven. Indeed, if one were to make judgments on the basis of speculation, one might guess that literature of the most pornographic sort would, in many cases, provide a substitute—not a stimulus—for antisocial sexual conduct. . . . As I read the First Amendment, judges cannot gear the literary diet of an entire nation to whatever tepid stuff is incapable of triggering the most demented mind. The First Amendment demands more than a horrible example or two of the perpetrator of a crime of sexual violence, in whose pocket is found a pornographic book, before it allows the Nation to be saddled with a regime of censorship. [According to a footnote: It would be a futile effort even for a censor to attempt to remove all that might possibly stimulate antisocial sexual conduct: "The majority [of individuals], needless to say, are somewhere between the over-scrupulous extremes of excitement and frigidity. . . . Within this variety, it is impossible to define 'hardcore' pornography, as if there were some singly lewd concept from which all profane ideas passed by imperceptible degrees into that sexuality called holy. But there is no 'hard-core.' Everything, every idea, is capable of being obscene if the personality perceiving it so apprehends it.

["It is for this reason that books, pictures, charades, ritual, the spoken word, *can* and *do* lead directly to conduct harmful to the self indulging in it and to others. Heinrich Pommerenke, who was a rapist, abuser, and mass slayer of women in Germany, was prompted to his series of ghastly deeds by Cecil B. DeMille's *The Ten Commandments*. During the scene of the Jewish women dancing about the Golden Calf, all the doubts of his life came clear: Women were the source of the world's trouble and it was his mission to both punish them for this and to execute them. Leaving the theater, he slew his first victim in a park nearby. John George Haigh, the British vampire who sucked his victims' blood through soda straws and dissolved their drained bodies in acid baths, first had his murder-inciting dreams and vampire-longings from watching the 'voluptuous' procedure of—an Anglican High Church Service!". . .]

> *Justice Thomas C. Clark, dissenting, held that* Fanny Hill *had been properly found obscene by the Massachusetts courts under applicable precedent and that the Massachusetts judgment should have been affirmed by the Supreme Court. He wrote:*

. . . [T]he public should know of the continuous flow of pornographic material reaching this Court and the increasing problem States have in controlling it. *Memoirs of a Woman of Pleasure*, the book involved here, is typical. I have "stomached" past cases for almost 10 years without much outcry. Though I am not known to be a purist—or a shrinking violet—this book is too much even for me. It is important that the Court has refused to declare it obscene and thus affords it further circulation. In order to give my remarks the proper setting I have been obliged to portray the book's contents, which causes me embarrassment. However, quotations from typical episodes would so debase our Reports that I will not follow that course.

I.

Let me first pinpoint the effect of today's holding in the obscenity field. While there is no majority opinion in this case, there are three Justices who import a new test into that laid down in *Roth* v. *United States*, . . . namely, that "[a] book cannot be proscribed unless it is found to be *utterly* without redeeming social value.". . . [S]uch a condition rejects the basic holding of *Roth* and gives the smut artist free rein to carry on his dirty business. My vote in that case—which was the deciding one for the majority opinion—was cast solely because the Court declared the test of obscenity to be: "whether to the average person, applying contemporary community standards, the dominant theme of the material taken as a whole appeals to prurient interest." I understood that test to include only two constitutional requirements: (1) the book must be judged as a whole, not by its parts; and (2) it must be judged in terms of its appeal to the prurient interest of the average person, applying contemporary community standards. Indeed, obscenity was denoted in *Roth* as having "*such slight social value as a step to truth that any benefit that may be derived . . . is clearly outweighed by the social interest in order and morality. . . .*" . . . Moreover, in no subsequent decision of this Court has any "utterly without redeeming social value" test been suggested, much less expounded. . . . The first reference to such a test was made by . . . [Justice] Brennan in *Jacobellis* v. *Ohio*, . . . seven years after *Roth*. In an opinion joined only by Justice [Arthur] Goldberg, he there wrote: "Recognizing that the test for obscenity enunciated [in *Roth*] . . . is not perfect, we think any substitute would raise equally difficult problems and we therefore adhere to that standard." Nevertheless, he proceeded to add: "We would reiterate, however, our recognition in *Roth* that obscenity is excluded from the constitutional protection only because it is 'utterly without redeeming social importance,' . . ."

This language was then repeated in the converse to announce this *non sequitur*: "It follows that material dealing with sex in a manner that advocates ideas . . . or that has literary or scientific or artistic value or any other form of social importance, may not be branded as obscenity and denied the constitutional protection.''. . .

Significantly no opinion in *Jacobellis*, other than that of my Brother Brennan, mentioned the ''utterly without redeeming social importance'' test which he there introduced into our many and varied previous opinions in obscenity cases. Indeed, rather than recognizing the ''utterly without social importance'' test, the chief justice [Earl Warren] in his dissent in *Jacobellis*, which I joined, specifically stated: ''In light of the foregoing, I would reiterate my acceptance of the rule of the *Roth* case: *Material is obscene and not constitutionally protected against regulation and proscription* if 'to the average person, applying contemporary community standards, the dominant theme of the material taken as a whole appeals to prurient interest.' '' (Emphasis added.) . . .

The Chief Justice and I further asserted that the enforcement of this rule should be committed to the state and federal courts whose judgments made pursuant to the *Roth* rule we would accept, limiting our review to a consideration of whether there is ''sufficient evidence'' in the record to support a finding of obscenity. . . .

II.

Three members of the majority hold that reversal here is necessary solely because their novel ''utterly without redeeming social value'' test was not properly interpreted or applied by the Supreme Judicial Court of Massachusetts. Massachusetts now has to retry the case although the ''Findings of Fact, Rulings of Law and Order for Final Decree'' of the trial court specifically held that ''this book is 'utterly without redeeming social importance' in the fields of art, literature, science, news or ideas of any social importance and that it is obscene, indecent and impure.'' I quote portions of the findings:

''Opinions of experts are admitted in evidence to aid the Court in its understanding and comprehension of the facts, but, of course, an expert cannot usurp the function of the Court. Highly artifical, stylistic writing and an abundance of metaphorical descriptions are contained in the book but the conclusions of some experts were pretty well strained in attempting to justify its claimed literary value: such as the book preached a moral that sex with love is better than sex without love, when Fanny's description of her sexual acts, particularly with the young boy she seduced, in Fanny's judgment at least, was to the contrary. *Careful review of all the expert testimony has been made*, but, the best evidence of all, is the book itself and it plainly has no value because of ideas, news or artistic, literary or scientific attributes. . . . Nor does it have any other merit. 'This Court will not adopt a rule of law which states obscenity is suppressible but well written obscenity is not.' Mr. Justice Scileppi in *People* v. *Fritch*. . . ." (Emphasis added.) . . .

None of these findings of the trial court were overturned on appeal, although the Supreme Judicial Court of Massachusetts observed in addition that "the fact that the testimony may indicate this book has some minimal literary value does not mean it is of any social importance. We do not interpret the 'social importance' test as requiring that a book which appeals to prurient interest and is patently offensive must be unqualifiedly worthless before it can be deemed obscene.". . .

In my view evidence of social importance is relevant to the determination of the ultimate question of obscenity. But social importance does not constitute a separate and distinct constitutional test. Such evidence must be considered together with evidence that the material in question appeals to prurient interest and is patently offensive . . .

III.

Memoirs is nothing more than a series of minutely and vividly described sexual episodes. The book starts with Fanny Hill, a young 15-year-old girl, arriving in London to seek household work. She goes to an employment office where through happenstance she meets the mistress of a bawdy house. This takes 10 pages. The remaining 200 pages of the book detail her initiation into various sexual experiences, from a lesbian encounter with a sister prostitute to all sorts and types of sexual debauchery in bawdy houses and as the mistress of a variety of men. This is presented to the reader through an uninterrupted succession of descriptions by Fanny, either as an observer or participant, of sexual adventures so vile that one of the male expert witnesses in the case was hesitant to repeat any one of them in the courtroom. These scenes run the gamut of possible sexual experience such as lesbianism, female masturbation, homosexuality between young boys, the destruction of a maidenhead with consequent gory descriptions, the seduction of a young virgin boy, the flagellation of male by female, and vice versa, followed by fervid sexual engagement, and other abhorrent acts, including over two dozen separate bizarre descriptions of different sexual intercourses between male and female characters. In one sequence four girls in a bawdy house are required in the presence of one another to relate the lurid details of their loss of virginity and their glorification of it. This is followed the same evening by "publick trials" in which each of the four girls engages in sexual intercourse with a different man while the others witness, with Fanny giving a detailed description of the movement and reaction of each couple.

In each of the sexual scenes the exposed bodies of the participants are described in minute and individual detail. The pubic hair is often used for a background to the most vivid and precise descriptions of the response, condition, size, shape, and color of the sexual organs before, during and after orgasms. There are some short transitory passages between the various sexual episodes, but for the most part they only set the scene and identify the participants for the next orgy, or make smutty reference and comparison to past episodes.

There can be no doubt that the whole purpose of the book is to arouse the prurient interest. Likewise the repetition of sexual episode after episode and the candor with which they are described renders the book "patently offensive." These facts weigh heavily in any appraisal of the book's claims to "redeeming social importance."

Let us now turn to evidence of the book's alleged social value. While unfortunately the State offered little testimony, the defense called several experts to attest that the book has literary merit and historical value. A careful reading of testimony, however, reveals that it has no substance. . . . If a book of art is one that asks for and receives a literary response, *Memoirs* is no work of art. The sole response evoked by the book is sensual. Nor does the orderly presentation of *Memoirs* make a difference; it presents nothing but lascivious scenes organized solely to arouse prurient interest and produce sustained erotic tension. Certainly the book's baroque style cannot vitiate the determination of obscenity. From a legal standpoint, we must remember that obscenity is no less obscene though it be expressed in "elaborate language.". . . To say that Fanny is an "intellectual" is an insult to those who travel under that tag. She was nothing but a harlot—a sensualist—exploiting her sexual attractions which she sold for fun, for money, for lodging and keep, for an inheritance, and finally for a husband. If she was curious about life, her curiosity extended only to the pursuit of sexual delight wherever she found it. The book describes nothing in the "external world" except bawdy houses and debaucheries. As an empiricist, Fanny confines her observations and "experiments" to sex, with primary attention to depraved, lewd, and deviant practices.

Other experts produced by the defense testified that the book emphasizes the profound "idea that a sensual passion is only truly experienced when it is associated with the emotion of love" and that the sexual relationship "can be a wholesome, healthy, experience itself," whereas in certain modern novels "the relationship between the sexes is seen as another manifestation of modern decadence, insterility or perversion." In my view this proves nothing as to social value. The state court properly gave such testimony no probative weight. A review offered by the defense noted that "where 'pornography' does not brutalize, it idealizes. The book is, in this sense, an erotic fantasy—and a male fantasy, at that, put into the mind of a woman. The male organ is phenomenal to the point of absurdity." Finally, it saw the book as "a minor fantasy, deluding as a guide to conduct, but respectful of our delight in the body . . . an interesting footnote in the history of the English novel." These unrelated assertions reveal to me nothing whatever of literary, historical, or social value. Another review called the book "a great novel . . . one which turns its convention upside down. . . ." Admittedly Cleland did not attempt "high art" because he was writing "an erotic novel. He can skip the elevation and get on with the erections." Fanny's "downfall" is seen as "one long delightful swoon into the depths of pleasurable sensation." Rather than indicating social value in the book, this evidence reveals just the contrary. Another item offered by the defense described *Memoirs* as being "widely accredited as the first deliberately dirty novel in English." However, the reviewer found Fanny to be "no common harlot. Her 'Memoirs' combine literary grace with a disarming enthusiasm for an activity which is, after all, only human. What is more, she never uses a dirty word." The short answer to such "expertise" is that none of these so-called attributes have any value to society. On the contrary, they accentuate the prurient appeal. . . .

The remaining experts testified in the same manner, claiming the book to be a "record of the historical, psychological, [and]

social events of the period." One has but to read the history of
the 18th century to disprove this assertion. The story depicts
nothing besides the brothels that are present in metropolitan cities in every period of history. . . .

It is, of course, the duty of the judge or the jury to determine
the question of obscenity, viewing the book by contemporary
community standards. It can accept the appraisal of experts or
discount their testimony in the light of the material itself or other
relevant testimony. So-called "literary obscenity," *i.e.*, the use
of erotic fantasies of the hard-core type clothed in an engaging
literary style has no constitutional protection. If a book deals
solely with erotic material in a manner calculated to appeal to
the prurient interest, it matters not that it may be expressed in
beautiful prose. There are obviously dynamic connections between art and sex—the emotional, intellectual, and physical—
but where the former is used solely to promote prurient appeal,
it cannot claim constitutional immunity. Cleland uses this technique to promote the prurient appeal of *Memoirs*. It is true that
Fanny's perverse experiences finally bring from her the observation that "the heights of [sexual] enjoyment cannot be achieved
until true affection prepares the bed of passion." But this merely emphasizes that sex, wherever and however found, remains
the sole theme of *Memoirs*. In my view, the book's repeated and
unrelieved appeals to the prurient interest of the average person
leave it utterly without redeeming social importance.

IV.

In his separate concurrence, my Brother Douglas asserts there
is no proof that obscenity produces antisocial conduct. I had
thought that this question was foreclosed by the determination
in *Roth* that obscenity was not protected by the First Amendment. I find it necessary to comment upon Brother Douglas'
views, however, because of the new requirement engrafted
upon *Roth* by Brother Brennan, *i.e.*, that material which "appeals to a prurient interest" and which is "patently offensive"
may still not be suppressed unless it is "utterly without redeeming social value." The question of antisocial effect thus becomes
relevant to the more limited question of social value. Brother
Brennan indicates that the social importance criterion encompasses only such things as the artistic, literary, and historical
qualities of the material. But the phrasing of the "utterly without
redeeming social value" test suggests that other evidence must

be considered. To say that social value may "redeem" implies that courts must balance alleged esthetic merit against the harmful consequences that may flow from pornography. Whatever the scope of the social value criterion . . . it at least anticipates that the trier of fact will weigh evidence of the material's influence in causing deviant or criminal conduct, particularly sex crimes, as well as its effect upon the mental, moral, and physical health of the average person. Brother Douglas' view as to the lack of proof in this area is not so firmly held among behavioral scientists as he would lead us to believe. For this reason, I should mention that there is a division of thought on the correlation between obscenity and socially deleterious behavior.

Psychological and physiological studies clearly indicate that many persons become sexually aroused from reading obscene material. [A footnote says: For a summary of experiments with various sexual stimuli see Cairns, Paul & Wishner, Sex Censorship: The Assumptions of Anti-Obscenity Laws and the Empirical Evidence, 46 Minn. L. Rev. 1009 (1962). The authors cite research by Kinsey disclosing that obscene literature stimulated a definite sexual response in a majority of the male and female subjects tested.]

While erotic stimulation caused by pornography may be legally insignificant in itself, there are medical experts who believe that such stimulation frequently manifests itself in criminal sexual behavior or other antisocial conduct. For example, Dr. George W. Henry of Cornell University has expressed the opinion that obscenity, with its exaggerated and morbid emphasis on sex, particularly abnormal and perverted practices, and its unrealistic presentation of sexual behavior and attitudes, may induce antisocial conduct by the average person. A number of sociologists think that this material may have adverse effects upon individual mental health, with potentially disruptive consequences for the community.

In addition, there is persuasive evidence from criminologists and police officials. Inspector Herbert Case of the Detroit Police Department contends that sex murder cases are invariably tied to some form of obscene literature. And the Director of the Federal Bureau of Investigation, J. Edgar Hoover, has repeatedly emphasized that pornography is associated with an overwhelmingly large number of sex crimes. Again, while the correlation between possession of obscenity and deviant behavior has not been conclusively established, the files of our law enforcement agencies contain many reports of persons who patterned their criminal conduct after behavior depicted in obscene material.

The clergy are also outspoken in their belief that pornography encourages violence, degeneracy and sexual misconduct. In a speech reported by the New York Journal-American August 7, 1964, Cardinal Spellman particularly stressed the direct influence obscenity has on immature persons. . . . After years of service with the West London Mission, Rev. Donald Soper found that pornography was a primary cause of prostitution. . . .

Congress and the legislatures of every State have enacted measures to restrict the distribution of erotic and pornographic material, justifying these controls by reference to evidence that antisocial behavior may result in part from reading obscenity. . . .

. . . I believe it can be established that the book "was commercially exploited for the sake of prurient appeal, to the exclusion of all other values" and should therefore be declared obscene under the test of commercial exploitation announced today in *Ginzburg* and *Mishkin*.

. . . [T]he record before the Court contains extrinsic evidence tending to show that the publisher was fully aware that the book attracted readers desirous of vicarious sexual pleasure, and sought to profit solely from its prurient appeal. The publisher's "Introduction" recites that Cleland, a "never-do-well bohemian," wrote the book in 1749 to make a quick 20 guineas. Thereafter, various publications of the book, often "embellished with fresh inflammatory details" and "highly exaggerated illustrations," appeared in "surreptitious circulation." Indeed, the cover of *Memoirs* tempts the reader with the announcement that the sale of the book has finally been permitted "after 214 years of suppression." Although written in a sophisticated tone, the "Introduction" repeatedly informs the reader that he may expect graphic descriptions of genitals and sexual exploits. For instance, it states: "Here and there, Cleland's descriptions of love-making are marred by what perhaps could be best described as his adherence to the 'longitudinal fallacy'—the formidable bodily equipment of his most accomplished lovers is apt to be described with quite unnecessary relish. . . .' Many other passages in the "Introduction" similarly reflect the publisher's "own evaluation" of the book's nature. The excerpt printed on the jacket of the hardcover edition is typical: "*Memoirs of a*

Woman of Pleasure is the product of a luxurious and licentious, but not a commercially degraded, era. . . . For all its abounding improprieties, his priapic novel is not a vulgar book. It treats of pleasure as the aim and end of existence, and of sexual satisfaction as the epitome of pleasure, but does so in a style that, despite its inflammatory subject, never stoops to a gross or unbecoming word."

Cleland apparently wrote only one other book, a sequel called *Memoirs of a Coxcomb*, published by Lancer Books, Inc. The "Introduction" to that book labels *Memoirs of a Woman of Pleasure* as "the most sensational piece of erotica in English literature." I daresay that this fact alone explains why G. P. Putman's Sons published this obscenity—preying upon prurient and carnal proclivities for its own pecuniary advantage. I would affirm the judgment.

> *Justice John Marshall Harlan, dissenting, criticized the lack of a court-devised "stable approach" to the issue. He held that the federal government and the states were not bound by identical restrictions in dealing with the problem. The federal government should suppress only "hardcore pornography," according to Harlan, but more flexible standards were desirable for the states. Harlan wrote:*

The central development that emerges from the aftermath of *Roth* v. *United States* . . . is that no stable approach to the obscenity problem has yet been devised by this Court. Two Justices believe that the First and Fourteenth Amendments absolutely protect obscene and nonobscene material alike. Another Justice believes that neither the State nor the Federal Government may suppress any material save for "hard-core pornography." *Roth* in 1957 stressed prurience and utter lack of redeeming social importance; as *Roth* has been expounded in this case, in *Ginzburg* v. *United States*, . . . and in *Mishkin* v. *New York*, . . . it has undergone significant transformation. The concept of "pandering" emphasized by the separate opinion of The Chief Justice in *Roth*, now emerges as an uncertain gloss or interpretive aid, and the further requisite of "patent offensiveness" has been made explicit as a result of intervening decisions. Given this tangled state of affairs, I feel free to adhere to the principles first set forth in my separate opinion in *Roth*. . . .

My premise is that in the area of obscenity the Constitution does not bind the States and the Federal Government in precisely the same fashion. . . . Although some 40 years have passed since the Court first indicated that the Fourteenth Amendment protects "free speech," see *Gitlow* v. *New York*, . . . the decisions have never declared that every utterance the Federal Government may not reach or every regulatory scheme it may not enact is also beyond the power of the State. The very criteria used in opinions to delimit the protection of free speech—the gravity of the evil being regulated, . . . how "clear and present" is the danger, . . . the magnitude of "such invasion of free speech as is necessary to avoid the danger," . . . —may and do depend on the particular context in which power is exercised. When, for example, the Court in *Beauharnais* v. *Illinois*, . . . upheld a criminal group-libel law because of the "social interest in order and morality," . . . it was acknowledging the responsibility and capacity of the States in such public-welfare matters and not committing itself to uphold any similar federal statute applying to such communications as Congress might otherwise regulate under the commerce power. . . .

Federal suppression of allegedly obscene matter should, in my view, be constitutionally limited to that often described as "hard-core pornography." To be sure, that rubric is not a self-executing standard, but it does describe something that most judges and others will "know . . . when [they] see it" (Stewart, J., in *Jacobellis* v. *Ohio*. . .) and that leaves the smallest room for disagreement between those of varying tastes. To me it is plain, for instance, that *Fanny Hill* does not fall within this class and could not be barred from the federal mails. If further articulation is meaningful, I would characterize as "hard-core" that prurient material that is patently offensive or whose indecency is self-demonstrating. . . . The Federal Government may be conceded a limited interest in excluding from the mails such gross pornography, almost universally condemned in this country. But I believe the dangers of national censorship and the existence of primary responsibility at the state level amply justify drawing the line at this point.

State obscenity laws present problems of quite a different order. The varying conditions across the country, the range of views on the need and reasons for curbing obscenity, and the traditions of local self-government in matters of public welfare all favor a far more flexible attitude in defining the bounds for the States. From my standpoint, the Fourteenth Amendment requires of a State only that it apply criteria rationally related to the accepted notion of obscenity and that it reach results not wholly out of step with current American standards. As to criteria, it should be adequate if the court or jury considers such elements as offensiveness, pruriency, social value, and the like. The latitude which I believe the States deserve cautions against any federally imposed formula listing the exclusive ingredients of obscenity and fixing their proportions. . . .

I believe the tests set out in the prevailing opinion, judged by their application in this case, offer only an illusion of certainty and risk confusion and prejudice. The opinion declares that a book cannnot be banned unless it is "utterly without redeeming social value." . . . To establish social value in the present case, a number of acknowledged experts in the field of literature testified that *Fanny Hill* held a respectable place in serious writing, and unless such largely uncontradicted testimony is accepted as decisive it is very hard to see that the "utterly without redeeming social value" test has any meaning at all. Yet the prevailing opinion, while denying that social value may be "weighted against" or "canceled by" prurience or offensiveness. . . , terminates this case unwilling to give a conclusive decision on the status of *Fanny Hill* under the Constitution. Apparently, the Court believes that the social value of the book may be negated if proof of pandering is present. Using this inherently vague "pandering" notion to offset "social value" wipes out any certainty the latter term might be given by reliance on experts, and admits into the case highly prejudicial evidence without appropriate restrictions. . . . I think it more satisfactory to acknowledge that on this record the book has been shown to have some quantum of social value, that it may at the same time be deemed offensive and salacious, and that the State's decision to weigh these elements and to ban this particular work does not exceed constitutional limits.

. . . Short of saying that no material relating to sex may be banned, or that all of it may be, I do not see how this Court can escape the task of reviewing obscenity decisions on a case-by-case basis. The views of literary or other experts could be made controlling, but those experts had their say in *Fanny Hill* and apparently the majority is no more willing than I to say that Massachusetts must abide by their verdict. Yet I venture to say that the Court's burden of decision would be ameliorated under the constitutional principles that I have advocated. "Hard-core pornography" for judging federal cases is one of the more tangible concepts in the field. As to the States, the due latitude my approach would leave them ensures that only the unusual case would require plenary review and correction by this Court. . . .

> *Justice Byron R. White, dissenting, objected that using "social importance" (in the sense indicated by the majority) as a test could bring such results as protecting "well written, especially effective obscenity" and making only "the poorly written . . . vulnerable." He wrote:*

In *Roth* v. *United States*, . . . the Court held a publication to be obscene if its predominant theme appeals to the prurient interest in a manner exceeding customary limits of candor. Material of this kind, the Court said, is "utterly without redeeming social importance" and is therefore unprotected by the First Amendment.

To say that material within the *Roth* definition of obscenity is nevertheless not obscene if it has some redeeming social value is to reject one of the basic propositions of the *Roth* case—that such material is not protected *because* it is inherently and utterly without social value.

If "social importance" is to be used as the prevailing opinion uses it today, obscene material, however far beyond customary limits of candor, is immune if it has any literary style, if it contains any historical references or language characteristic of a bygone day, or even if it is printed or bound in an interesting way. Well written, especially effective obscenity is protected; the poorly written is vulnerable. And why shouldn't the fact that some people buy and read such material prove its "social value"?

A fortiori, if the predominant theme of the book appeals to the prurient interest as stated in *Roth* but the book nevertheless contains here and there a passage descriptive of character, geography or architecture, the book would not be "obscene" under the social importance test. I had thought that *Roth* counseled the contrary: that the character of the book is fixed by its predominant theme and is not altered by the presence of minor themes of a different nature. The *Roth* Court's emphatic reliance on the quotation from *Chaplinsky* v. *New Hampshire* . . . means nothing less: "'. . . There are certain well-defined and narrowly limited classes of speech, the prevention and punishment of which have never been thought to raise any Constitutional problem. *These include the lewd and obscene. . . . It has been well observed that such utterances are no essential part of any exposition of ideas, and are of such slight social value as a step to truth that any benefit that may be derived from them is clearly outweighed by the social interest in order and morality. . . .* (Emphasis added.)". . .

In my view, "social importance" is not an independent test of obscenity but is relevant only to determining the predominant prurient interest of the material, a determination which the court or the jury will make based on the material itself and all the evidence in the case, expert or otherwise.

Application of the *Roth* test, as I understand it, necessarily involves the exercise of judgment by legislatures, courts and juries. But this does not mean that there are no limits to what may be done in the name of *Roth*. . . . *Roth* does not mean that a legislature is free to ban books simply because they deal with sex or because they appeal to the prurient interest. Nor does it mean that if books like *Fanny Hill* are unprotected, their nonprurient appeal is necessarily lost to the world. Literary style, history, teachings about sex, character description (even of a prostitute) or moral lessons need not come wrapped in such packages. The fact that they do impeaches their claims to immunity from legislative censure.

Finally, it should be remembered that if the publication and sale of *Fanny Hill* and like books are proscribed, it is not the Constitution that imposes the ban. Censure stems from a legislative act, and legislatures are constitutionally free to embrace such books whenever they wish to do so. But if a State insists on treating *Fanny Hill* as obscene and forbidding its sale, the First Amendment does not prevent it from doing so. . . .

Ginsberg Case Backs Stricter Rules for Children

> *The Supreme Court ruled April 22, 1968, in the case of* Ginsberg v. New York, *that states had a right to bar to minors the sale of items that were not barred to adults. The court's opinion, delivered by Justice William J. Brennan Jr., upheld the conviction of New York storekeeper Sam Gins-*

berg who had sold "girlie" magazines to a 16-year-old boy; such literature could be sold at that time without penalty to adults. Brennan wrote:

This case presents the question of the constitutionality on its face of a New York criminal obscenity statute which prohibits the sale to minors under 17 years of age of material defined to be obscene on the basis of its appeal to them whether or not it would be obscene to adults.

Appellant and his wife operate "Sam's Stationery and Luncheonette" in Bellmore, Long Island. They have a lunch counter, and, among other things, also sell magazines including some so-called "girlie" magazines. Appellant was prosecuted under two informations, each in two counts, which charged that he personally sold a 16-year-old boy two "girlie" magazines on each of two dates in October 1965, in violation of § 484-h of the New York Penal Law. He . . . was found guilty on both counts. The judge found (1) that the magazines contained pictures which depicted female "nudity" in a manner defined in subsection 1 (b), that is "the showing of . . . female . . . buttocks with less than a full opaque covering, or the showing of the female breast with less than a fully opaque covering of any portion thereof below the top of the nipple . . . ," and (2) that the pictures were "harmful to minors" in that they had, within the meaning of subsection 1 (f) "that quality of . . . representation . . . of nudity . . . [which] . . . (i) predominantly appeals to the prurient, shameful or morbid interest of minors, and (ii) is patently offensive to prevailing standards in the adult community as a whole with respect to what is suitable material for minors, and (iii) is utterly without redeeming social importance for minors." He held that both sales to the 16-year-old boy therefore constituted the violation under § 484-h of "knowingly to sell . . . to a minor" under 17 of "(a) any picture . . . which depicts nudity . . . and which is harmful to minors," and "(b) any . . . magazine . . . which contains . . . [such pictures] . . . and which, taken as a whole, is harmful to minors." The conviction was affirmed . . . by the Appellate Term, Second Department, of the Supreme Court. . . . We affirm.

I.

The "girlie" picture magazines involved in the sales here are not obscene for adults, *Redrup v. New York.* . . . [A footnote cited court decisions indicating that magazines of this type, including a different issue of one of the magazines in the case, were not obscene.] But § 484-h does not bar the appellant from stocking the magazines and selling them to persons 17 years of age or older, and therefore the conviction is not invalid under our decision in *Butler* v. *Michigan.* . . .

Obscenity is not within the area of protected speech or press. *Roth* v. *United States* . . . The three-pronged test of subsection 1(f) for judging the obscenity of material sold to minors under 17 is a variable from the formulation for determining obscenity under *Roth* stated in the plurality opinion in *Memoirs* v. *Massachusetts.* . . . Appellant's primary attack upon § 484-h is leveled at the power of the State to adapt this *Memoirs* formulation to define the material's obscenity on the basis of its appeal to minors, and thus exclude material so defined from the area of protected expression. He makes no argument that the magazines are not "harmful to minors" within the definition in subsection 1 (f). . . .

The New York Court of Appeals "upheld the Legislature's power to employ variable concepts of obscenity" [a footnote quotes Lockhart & McClure, Censorship of Obscenity: The Developing Constitutional Standards, 45 Minn. L. Rev. 5 (1960), as saying: "variable obscenity . . . furnishes a useful analytical tool for dealing with the problem of denying adolescents access to material aimed at a primary audience of sexually mature adults. For variable obscenity focuses attention upon the makeup of primary and peripheral audiences in varying circumstances, and provides a reasonably satisfactory means for delineating the obscene in each circumstance"] in a case in which the same challenge to state power to enact such a law was also addressed to § 484-h. . . . In sustaining state power to enact the law, the Court of Appeals said, *Bookcase, Inc.* v. *Broderick* . . .: "[M]aterial which is protected for distribution to adults is not necessarily constitutionally protected from restriction upon its dissemination to children. In other words, the concept of obscenity or of unprotected matter may vary according to the group to whom the questionable material is directed or from whom it is quarantined. Because of the State's exigent interest in preventing distribution to children of objectionable material, it can exercise its power to protect the health, safety, welfare and morals of its community by barring the distribution to children of books recognized to be suitable for adults."

Appellant's attack is not that New York was without power to draw the line at age 17. Rather, his contention is the broad proposition that the scope of the constitutional freedom of expression secured to a citizen to read or see material concerned with sex cannot be made to depend upon whether the citizen is an adult or a minor. He accordingly insists that the denial to minors under 17 of access to material condemned by § 484–h, insofar as that material is not obscene for persons 17 years of age or older, constitutes an unconstitutional deprivation of protected liberty.

. . . It is enough for the purposes of this case that we inquire whether it was constitutionally impermissible for New York, insofar as § 484–h does so, to accord minors under 17 a more restricted right than that assured to adults to judge and determine for themselves what sex material they may read or see. We conclude that we cannot say that the statute invades the area of freedom of expression constitutionally secured to minors. [A footnote says that "the obscenity laws of 35 other States include provisions referring to minors."]

Appellant argues that there is an invasion of protected rights under § 484–h constitutionally indistinguishable from the invasions under the Nebraska statute forbidding children to study German, which was struck down in *Meyer* v. *Nebraska* . . . ; the Oregon statute interfering with children's attendance at private and parochial schools, which was struck down in *Pierce* v. *Society of Sisters* . . . ; and the statute compelling children against their religious scruples to give the flag salute, which was struck down in *West Virginia State Board of Education* v. *Barnette*. . . . We reject that argument. We do not regard New York's regulation in defining obscenity on the basis of its appeal to minors under 17 as involving an invasion of such minors' constitutionally protected freedoms. Rather § 484–h simply adjusts the definition of obscenity "to social realities by permitting the appeal of this type of material to be assessed in terms of the sexual interests . . ." of such minors. *Mishkin* v. *New York* . . . ; *Bookcase, Inc.* v. *Broderick*. . . . That the State has power to make that adjustment seems clear, for we have recognized that even where there is an invasion of protected freedoms "the power of the state to control the conduct of children reaches beyond the scope of its authority over adults . . . ." *Prince* v. *Massachusetts*. . . . [According to a footnote, many commentators, including many committed to the proposition that "[n]o general restriction on expression in terms of 'obscenity' can . . . be reconciled with the first amendment," recognize that "the power of the state to control the conduct of children reaches beyond the scope of its authority over adults," and accordingly acknowledge a supervening state interest in the regulation of literature sold to children, Emerson, Toward a General Theory of the First Amendment, 72 Yale L. J. 877, 938, 939 (1963): "Different factors come into play, also, where the interest at stake is the effect of erotic expression upon children. The world of children is not strictly part of the adult realm of free expression. The factor of immaturity, and perhaps other considerations, impose different rules. Without attempting here to formulate the principles relevant to freedom of expression for children, it suffices to say that regulations of communication addressed to them need not conform to the requirements of the first amendment in the same way as those applicable to adults." . . .] . . .

The well-being of its children is of course a subject within the State's constitutional power to regulate, and, in our view, two interests justify the limitations in § 484–h upon the availability of sex material to minors under 17, at least if it was rational for the legislature to find that the minors' exposure to such material might be harmful. First of all, constitutional interpretation has consistently recognized that the parents' claim to authority in their own household to direct the rearing of their children is basic in the structure of our society. . . . The legislature could properly conclude that parents and others, teachers for example, who have this primary responsibility for children's well-being are entitled to the support of laws designed to aid discharge of that responsibility. Indeed, subsection 1 (f) (ii) of § 484–h expressly recognizes the parental role in assessing sex-related material harmful to minors according "to prevailing standards in the adult community as a whole with respect to what is suitable material for minors." Moreover, the prohibition against sales to minors does not bar parents who so desire from purchasing the magazines for their children.

The State also has an independent interest in the well-being of its youth. The New York Court of Appeals squarely bottomed its decision on that interest in *Bookcase, Inc.* v. *Broderick.* . . . Judge Fuld, now Chief Judge Fuld, also emphasized its significance in the earlier case of *People* v. *Kahan,* . . . which had struck down the first version of § 484–h on grounds of vagueness. In his concurring opinion, . . . he said: "While the supervision of children's reading may best be left to their parents, the knowledge that parental control or guidance cannot always be provided and society's transcendent interest in protecting the welfare of children justify reasonable regulation of the sale of material to them. It is, therefore, altogether fitting and proper for a state to include in a statute designed to regulate the sale of pornography to children special standards, broader than those embodied in legislation aimed at controlling dissemination of such material to adults." In *Prince* v. *Massachusetts, supra,* at 165, this Court, too, recognized that the State has an interest "to protect the welfare of children" and to see that they are "safeguarded from abuses" which might prevent their "growth into free and independent well-developed men and citizens." The only question remaining, therefore, is whether the New York Legislature might rationally conclude, as it has, that exposure to the materials proscribed by § 484–h constitutes such an "abuse."

Section 484–e of the law states a legislative finding that the material condemned by § 484–h is "a basic factor in impairing the ethical and moral development of our youth and a clear and present danger to the people of the state." It is very doubtful that this finding expresses an accepted scientific fact. But obscenity is not protected expression and may be suppressed without a showing of the circumstances which lie behind the phrase "clear and present danger" in its application to protected speech. *Roth* v. *United States.* . . . To sustain state power to exclude material defined as obscenity by § 484–h requires only that we be able to say that it was not irrational for the legislature to find that exposure to material condemned by the statute is harmful to minors. In *Meyer* v. *Nebraska,* . . . we were able to say that children's knowledge of the German language "cannot reasonably be regarded as harmful." That cannot be said by us of minors' reading and seeing sex material. To be sure, there is no lack of "studies" which purport to demonstrate that obscenity is or is not "a basic factor in impairing the ethical and moral development of . . . youth and a clear and present danger to the people of the state." But the growing consensus of commentators is that "while these studies all agree that a causal link has not been demonstrated, they are equally agreed that a causal link has not been disproved either." We do not demand of legislatures "scientifically certain criteria of legislation." *Noble State*

Bank v. *Haskell.* . . . We therefore cannot say that § 484–h, in defining the obscenity of material on the basis of its appeal to minors under 17, has no rational relation to the objective of safeguarding such minors from harm.

II

Appellant challenges subsections (f) and (g) of § 484–h as in any event void for vagueness. The attack on subsection (f) is that the definition of obscenity "harmful to minors" is so vague that an honest distributor of publications cannot know when he might be held to have violated § 484–h. But the New York Court of Appeals construed this definition to be "virtually identical to the Supreme Court's most recent statement of the elements of obscenity. . . . The definition therefore gives "men in acting adequate notice of what is prohibited" and does not offend the requirements of due process. . . .

As is required by *Smith* v. *California,* . . . § 484–h prohibits only those sales made "knowingly." The challenge to the *scienter* requirement of subsection (g) centers on the definition of "knowingly" insofar as it includes "reason to know" or "a belief or ground for belief which warrants further inspection or inquiry of both: (i) the character and content of any material described herein which is reasonably susceptible of examination by the defendant, and (ii) the age of the minor, provided however, that an honest mistake shall constitute an excuse from liability hereunder if the defendant made a reasonable bona fide attempt to ascertain the true age of such minor."

As to (i), § 484–h was passed after the New York Court of Appeals decided *People* v. *Finkelstein,* . . . which read the requirement of *scienter* into New York's general obscenity statute, § 1141 of the Penal Law. The constitutional requirement of *scienter,* in the sense of knowledge of the contents of material, rests on the necessity "to avoid the hazard of self-censorship of constitutionally protected material and to compensate for the ambiguities inherent in the definition of obscenity," *Mishkin* v. *New York.* . . . The Court of Appeals in *Finkelstein* interpreted § 1141 to require "the vital element of scienter" and defined that requirement in these terms: "A reading of the statute [§ 1141] as a whole clearly indicates that only those who are *in some manner aware of the character of the material* they attempt to distribute should be punished. It is not innocent but *calculated* purveyance of filth which is exorcised. . . ." . . . (Emphasis supplied.)

In *Mishkin* v. *New York*, . . . we held that a challenge to the validity of § 1141 founded on *Smith* v. *California, supra*, was foreclosed in light of this construction. When § 484–h was before the New York Legislature its attention was directed to *People* v. *Finkelstein*, as defining the nature of *scienter* required to sustain the statute. . . . We may therefore infer that the reference in provision (i) to knowledge of "the *character* and content of any material described herein" incorporates the gloss given the term "characrer" in *People* v. *Finkelstein*. In that circumstance *Mishkin* requires rejection of appellant's challenge to provision (i) and makes it unnecessary for us to define further today "what sort of mental element is requisite to a constitutionally permissible prosecution," *Smith* v. *California*. . . . *Affirmed.*

APPENDIX A TO OPINION OF THE COURT.

New York Penal Law § 484–h as enacted oy L. 1965, c. 327, provides: § 484–h. Exposing minors to harmful materials
1. Definitions. As used in this section:
(a) "Minor" means any person under the age of seventeen years.
(b) "Nudity" means the showing of the human male or female genitals, pubic area or buttocks with less than a full opaque covering, or the showing of the female breast with less than a fully opaque covering of any portion thereof below the top of the nipple, or the depiction of covered male genitals in a discernibly turgid state.
(c) "Sexual conduct" means acts of masturbation, homosexuality, sexual intercourse, or physical contact with a person's clothed or unclothed genitals, pubic area, buttocks or, if such person be a female, breast.
(d) "Sexual excitement" means the condition of human male or female genitals when in a state of sexual stimulation or arousal.
(e) "Sado-masochistic abuse" means flagellation or torture by or upon a person clad in undergarments, a mask or bizarre costume, or the condition of being fettered, bound or otherwise physically restrained on the part of one so clothed.
(f) "Harmful to minors" means that quality of any description or representation, in whatever form, of nudity, sexual conduct, sexual excitement, or sado-masochistic abuse, when it:
(i) predominantly appeals to the prurient, shameful or morbid interest of minors, and

(ii) is patently offensive to prevailing standards in the adult community as a whole with respect to what is suitable material for minors, and

(iii) is utterly without redeeming social importance for minors.

(g) "Knowingly" means having general knowledge of, or reason to know, or a belief or ground for belief which warrants further inspection or inquiry of both:

(i) the character and content of any material described herein which is reasonably susceptible of examination by the defendant, and

(ii) the age of the minor, provided however, that an honest mistake shall constitute an excuse from liability hereunder if the defendant made a reasonable bona fide attempt to ascertain the true age of such minor.

2. It shall be unlawful for any person knowingly to sell or loan for monetary consideration to a minor:

(a) any picture, photograph, drawing, sculpture, motion picture film, or similar visual representation or image of a person or portion of the human body which depicts nudity, sexual conduct or sado-masochistic abuse and which is harmful to minors, or

(b) any book, pamphlet, magazine, printed matter however reproduced, or sound recording which contains any matter enumerated in paragraph (a) of subdivision two hereof, or explicit and detailed verbal descriptions or narrative accounts of sexual excitement, sexual conduct or sado-masochistic abuse and which, taken as a whole, is harmful to minors.

3. It shall be unlawful for any person knowingly to exhibit for a monetary consideration to a minor or knowingly to sell to a minor an admission ticket or pass or knowingly to admit a minor for a monetary consideration to premises whereon there is exhibited, a motion picture, show or other presentation which, in whole or in part, depicts nudity, sexual conduct or sado-masochistic abuse and which is harmful to minors. . . .

Miller Ruling Tightens Rules

In the case of Miller v. California, *decided by the Supreme Court June 21, 1973, the court tightened restrictions against alleged obscenity. The test of* "utterly *without redeeming social value" was rejected, and local rather than national standards*

*were permitted. The court reversed the conviction
of a California defendant who had been found
guilty of violating a state law by mailing unsolicited sexually explicit material. Chief Justice Warren
E. Burger, delivering the opinion of the court,
wrote:*

This is one of a group of "obscenity-pornography" cases being reviewed by the Court in a re-examination of standards
enunciated in earlier cases involving what Mr. Justice Harlan
called "the intractable obscenity problem." . . .

Appellant conducted a mass mailing campaign to advertise the
sale of illustrated books, euphemistically called "adult" material. After a jury trial, he was convicted of violating California
Penal Code §311.2(a), a misdemeanor, by knowingly distributing
obscene matter. . . .

[The footnote said: At the time of the commission of the alleged offense, which was prior to June 25, 1969, §§311.2(a) and
311 of the California Penal Code read in relevant part:

["§311.2 . . . (a) Every person who knowingly: sends or
causes to be sent, or brings or causes to be brought, into this
state for sale or distribution, or in this state prepares, publishes,
prints, exhibits, distributes, or offers to distribute, or has in his
possession with intent to distribute or to exhibit or offer to distribute, any obscene matter is guilty of a misdemeanor. . . ."

["§311. Definitions. "As used in this chapter: (a) 'Obscene'
means that to the average person, applying contemporary standards, the predominant appeal of the matter, taken as a whole, is
to prurient interest, i.e., a shameful or morbid interest in nudity,
sex, or excretion, which goes substantially beyond customary
limits of candor in description or representation of such matters
and is matter which is utterly without redeeming social importance. (b) 'Matter' means any book, magazine, newspaper, or
other printed or written material or any picture, drawing, photograph, motion picture, or other pictorial representation or any
statue or other figure, or any recording, transcription or me-
chanical, chemical or electrical reproduction or any other articles, equipment, machines or materials . . . (d) 'Distribute'
means to transfer possession of, whether with or without consideration. (e) 'Knowingly' means having knowledge that the
matter is obscene."

[Section 311(e) of the California Penal Code, *supra*, was
amended on June 25, 1969, to read as follows: "(e) 'Knowingly'

means being aware of the character of the matter.''] Appellant's conviction was specifically based on his conduct in causing five unsolicited advertising brochures to be sent through the mail in an envelope addressed to a restaurant in Newport Beach, California. The envelope was opened by the manager of the restaurant and his mother. They had not requested the brochures; they complained to the police.

The brochures advertise four books entitled "Intercourse," "Man-Woman," "Sex Orgies Illustrated," and "An Illustrated History of Pornography," and a film entitled "Marital Intercourse." While the brochures contain some descriptive printed material, primarily they consist of pictures and drawings very explicitly depicting men and women in groups of two or more engaging in a variety of sexual activities, with genitals often prominently displayed.

I

This case involves the application of a State's criminal obscenity statute to a situation in which sexually explicit materials have been thrust by aggressive sales action upon unwilling recipients who had in no way indicated any desire to receive such materials. This Court has recognized that the States have a legitimate interest in prohibiting dissemination or exhibition of obscene material when the mode of dissemination carries with it a significant danger of offending the sensibilities of unwilling recipients or of exposure to juveniles. . . . It is in this context that we are called on to define the standards which must be used to identify obscene material that a State may regulate without infringing on the First Amendment as applicable to the States through the Fourteenth Amendment.

The dissent of Mr. Justice Brennan reviews the background of the obscenity problem, but since the Court now undertakes to formulate standards more concrete than those in the past, it is useful for us to focus on two of the landmark cases in the somewhat tortured history of the Court's obscenity decisions. In *Roth* v. *United States* . . . (1957), the Court sustained a conviction under a federal statute punishing the mailing of "obscene, lewd, lascivious or filthy . . ." materials. The key to that holding was the Court's rejection of the claim that obscene materials were protected by the First Amendment. Five Justices joined in the opinion stating:

"All ideas having even the slightest redeeming social importance—unorthodox ideas, controversial ideas, even ideas hateful to the prevailing climate of opinion—have the full protection of the [First Amendment] guaranties, unless excludable because they encroach upon the limited area of more important interests. But implicit in the history of the First Amendment is the rejection of obscenity as utterly without redeeming social importance. . . .

" '. . . There are certain well-defined and narrowly limited classes of speech, the prevention and punishment of which have never been thought to raise any Constitutional problem. *These include the lewd and obscene. . . . It has been well observed that such utterances are no essential part of any exposition of ideas, and are of such slight social value as a step to truth that any benefit that may be derived from them is clearly outweighed by the social interest in order and morality. . . .*' [Emphasis by Court in *Roth* opinion.]

"We hold that obscenity is not within the area of constitutionally protected speech or press." . . .

Nine years later, in *Memoirs* v. *Massachusetts* . . . (1966), the Court veered sharply away from the *Roth* concept and, with only three Justices in the plurality opinion, articulated a new test of obscenity. The plurality held that under the *Roth* definition "as elaborated in subsequent cases, three elements must coalesce: it must be established that (a) the dominant theme of the material taken as a whole appeals to a prurient interest in sex; (b) the material is patently offensive because it affronts contemporary community standards relating to the description or representation of sexual matters; and (c) the material is utterly without redeeming social value." . . .

The sharpness of the break with *Roth*, represented by the third element of the *Memoirs* test and emphasized by Mr. Justice White's dissent, . . . was further underscored when the *Memoirs* plurality went on to state: "The Supreme Judicial Court erred in holding that a book need not be 'unqualifiedly worthless before it can be deemed obscene.' A book cannot be proscribed unless it is found to be *utterly* without redeeming social value." . . . (emphasis in original).

While *Roth* presumed "obscenity" to be "utterly without redeeming social importance," *Memoirs* required that to prove obscenity it must be affirmatively established that the material is "*utterly* without redeeming social value." Thus, even as they repeated the words of *Roth,* the *Memoirs* plurality produced a drastically altered test that called on the prosecution to prove a negative, *i. e.,* that the material was "*utterly* without redeeming social value"—a burden virtually impossible to discharge under our criminal standards of proof. Such considerations caused Mr. Justice Harlan to wonder if the "*utterly* without redeeming social value" test had any meaning at all. . . .

Apart from the initial formulation in the *Roth* case, no majority of the Court has at any given time been able to agree on a standard to determine what constitutes obscene, pornographic material subject to regulation under the States' police power. . . . We have seen "a variety of views among the members of the Court unmatched in any other course of consitutional adjudication." . . . [A footnote says: In the absence of a majority view, this Court was compelled to embark on the practice of summarily reversing convictions for the dissemination of materials that at least five members of the Court, applying their separate tests, found to be protected by the First Amendment. *Redrup* v. *New York* . . . (1967). Thirty-one cases have been decided in this manner. Beyond the necessity of circumstances, however, no justification has ever been offered in support of the *Redrup* "policy." The *Redrup* procedure has cast us in the role of an unreviewable board of censorship for the 50 States, subjectively judging each piece of material brought before us.] This is not remarkable, for in the area of freedom of speech and press the courts must always remain sensitive to any infringement on genuinely serious literary, artistic, political, or scientific expression. This is an area in which there are few eternal verities.

The case we now review was tried on the theory that the California Penal Code § 311 approximately incorporates the three-stage *Memoirs* test. . . . But now the *Memoirs* test has been abandoned as unworkable by its author, and no Member of the Court today supports the *Memoirs* formulation.

II

This much has been categorically settled by the Court, that obscene material is unprotected by the First Amendment. *Kois* v. *Wisconsin* . . . (1972); *United States* v. *Reidel* . . .; *Roth* v. *United States.* . . . [A footnote says: As Mr. Chief Justice Warren stated, dissenting, in *Jacobellis* v. *Ohio* . . . (1964): "For all the sound and fury that the *Roth* test has generated, it has not been proved unsound, and I believe that we should try to live with it—at least until a more satisfactory definition is evolved. No government—be it federal, state, or local—should be forced to choose between repressing all material, including that within the realm of decency, and allowing unrestrained license to publish any material, no matter how vile. There must be a rule of reason in this as in other areas of the law, and we have attempted in the *Roth* case to provide such a rule.''] ''The First and Fourteenth Amendments have never been treated as absolutes . . . .'' *Breard* v. *Alexandria* . . . and cases cited. See *Times Film Corp.* v. *Chicago* . . .; *Joseph Burstyn, Inc.* v. *Wilson.* . . . We acknowledge, however, the inherent dangers of undertaking to regulate any form of expression. State statutes designed to regulate obscene materials must be carefully limited. . . . As a result, we now confine the permissible scope of such regulation to works which depict or describe sexual conduct. That conduct must be specifically defined by the applicable state law, as written or authoritatively construed. [A footnote cites Oregon and Hawaiian laws ''as examples of state laws directed at depiction of defined physical conduct, as opposed to expression.'' The footnote adds: ''Other state formulations could be equally valid in this respect. In giving the Oregon and Hawaii statutes as examples, we do not wish to be understood as approving of them in all other respects nor as establishing their limits as the extent of state power. We do not hold, as Mr. Justice Brennan intimates, that all States other than Oregon must now enact new obscenity statutes. Other existing state statutes, as construed heretofore or hereafter, may well be adequate. . . .''] A state offense must also be limited to works which, taken as a whole, appeal to the prurient interest in sex, which portray sexual conduct in a patently offensive way, and which, taken as a whole, do not have serious literary, artistic, political, or scientific value.

The basic guidelines for the trier of fact must be: (a) whether ''the average person, applying contemporary community standards'' would find that the work, taken as a whole, appeals to the prurient interest . . .; (b) whether the work depicts or describes, in a patently offensive way, sexual conduct specifically defined by the applicable state law; and (c) whether the work, taken as a whole, lacks serious literary, artistic, political, or scientific value. We do not adopt as a constitutional standard the ''*utterly* without redeeming social value'' test of *Memoirs* v. *Massachusetts* . . .; that concept has never commanded the adherence of more than three Justices at one time. [According to a footnote: "A quotation from Voltaire in the flyleaf of a book will not constitutionally redeem an otherwise obscene publication. . . ." *Kois* v. *Wisconsin* . . . (1972). . . . We also reject, as a constitutional standard, the ambiguous concept of "social importance." . . .] . . . If a state law that regulates obscene material is thus limited, as written or construed, the First Amendment values applicable to the States through the Fourteenth Amendment are adequately protected by the ultimate power of appellate courts to conduct an independent review of constitutional claims when necessary. . . .

We emphasize that it is not our function to propose regulatory schemes for the States. That must await their concrete legislative efforts. It is possible, however, to give a few plain examples of what a state statute could define for regulation under part (b) of the standard announced in this opinion, *supra:*

(a) Patently offensive representations or descriptions of ultimate sexual acts, normal or perverted, actual or simulated.

(b) Patently offensive representations or descriptions of masturbation, excretory functions, and lewd exhibition of the genitals.

Sex and nudity may not be exploited without limit by films or pictures exhibited or sold in places of public accommodation any more than live sex and nudity can be exhibited or sold without limit in such public places. [A footnote adds: Although we are not presented here with the problem of regulating lewd public conduct itself, the States have greater power to regulate nonverbal, physical conduct than to suppress depictions or descriptons of the same behavior. In *United States* v. *O'Brien* . . . (1968), a case not dealing with obscenity, the Court held a State regulation of conduct which itself embodied both speech and nonspeech elements to be "sufficiently justified if . . . it furthers an important or substantial governmental interest; if the governmental interest is unrelated to the suppression of free expression; and if the incidental restriction on alleged First Amendment freedoms is no greater than is essential to the furtherance of that interest." . . .] At a minimum, prurient, patently offensive depiction or description of sexual conduct must have serious literary, artistic, political, or scientific value to merit First Amendment protection. . . . For example, medical books for the education of physicians and related personnel necessarily use graphic illustrations and descriptions of human anatomy. In resolving the inevitably sensitive questions of fact and law, we must continue to rely on the jury system, accompanied by the safeguards that judges, rules of evidence, presumption of innocence, and other protective features provide, as we do with rape, murder, and a host of other offenses against society and its individual members.

Mr. Justice Brennan, author of the opinions of the Court, or the plurality opinions, in *Roth* v. *United States* . . .; *Jacobellis* v. *Ohio* . . .; *Ginzburg* v. *United States* . . .; *Mishkin* v. *New York* . . .; and *Memoirs* v. *Massachusetts* . . . has abandoned his former position and now maintains that no formulation of this Court, the Congress, or the States can adequately distinguish obscene material unprotected by the First Amendment from protected expression, *Paris Adult Theatre I* v. *Slaton*. . . . Paradoxically, Mr. Justice Brennan indicates that suppression of unprotected obscene material is permissible to avoid exposure to unconsenting adults, as in this case, and to juveniles, although he gives no indication of how the division between protected and nonprotected materials may be drawn with greater precision for these purposes than for regulation of commercial exposure to consenting adults only. Nor does he indicate where in the Constitution he finds the authority to distinguish between a willing "adult" one month past the state law age of majority and a willing "juvenile" one month younger.

Under the holdings announced today, no one will be subject to prosecution for the sale or exposure of obscene materials unless these materials depict or describe patently offensive "hard core" sexual conduct specifically defined by the regulating state law, as written or construed. We are satisfied that these specific prerequisites will provide fair notice to a dealer in such materials that his public and commercial activities may bring prosecution. . . . If the inability to define regulated materials with ultimate, god-like precision altogether removes the power of the States or the Congress to regulate, then "hard core" pornography may be exposed without limit to the juvenile, the passerby, and the consenting adult alike, as, indeed, Mr. Justice Douglas contends. . . . In this belief, however, Mr. Justice Douglas now stands alone.

Mr. Justice Brennan also emphasizes "institutional stress" in justification of his change of view. Noting that "[t]he number of obscenity cases on our docket gives ample testimony to the burden that has been placed upon this Court," he quite rightly remarks that the examination of contested materials "is hardly a source of edification to the members of this Court." *Paris Adult Theatre I* v. *Slaton*. . . . He also notes, and we agree, that "uncertainty of the standards creates a continuing source of tension between state and federal courts. . . ." "The problem is . . . that one cannot say with certainty that material is obscene until at least five members of this Court, applying inevitably obscure standards, have pronounced it so."

It is certainly true that the absence, since *Roth*, of a single majority view of this Court as to proper standards for testing obscenity has placed a strain on both state and federal courts. But today, for the first time since *Roth* was decided in 1957, a majority of this Court has agreed on concrete guidelines to isolate "hard core" pornography from expression protected by the First Amendment. Now we may abandon the casual practice of *Redrup* v. *New York* . . . and attempt to provide positive guidance to federal and state courts alike.

This may not be an easy road, free from difficulty. But no amount of "fatigue" should lead us to adopt a convenient "institutional" rationale—an absolutist, "anything goes" view of the First Amendment—because it will lighten our burdens. "Such an abnegation of judicial supervision in this field would be inconsistent with our duty to uphold the constitutional guarantees." *Jacobellis* v. *Ohio* . . . (opinion of Brennan, J.). Nor should we remedy "tension between state and federal courts" by arbitrarily depriving the States of a power reserved to them under the Constitution, a power which they have enjoyed and exercised continuously from before the adoption of the First Amendment to this day. . . . "Our duty admits of no 'substitute for facing up to the tough individual problems of constitutional judgment involved in every obscenity case.' . . ." *Jacobellis* v. *Ohio* . . . (opinion of Brennan, J.).

III

Under a National Constitution, fundamental First Amendment limitations on the powers of the States do not vary from community to community, but this does not mean that there are, or should or can be, fixed, uniform national standards of precisely what appeals to the "prurient interest" or is "patently offensive." These are essentially questions of fact, and our Nation is simply too big and too diverse for this Court to reasonably expect that such standards could be articulated for all 50 States in a single formulation, even assuming the prerequisite consensus exists. When triers of fact are asked to decide whether "the average person, applying contemporary community standards" would consider certain materials "prurient," it would be unrealistic to require that the answer be based on some abstract formulation. The adversary system, with lay jurors as the usual ultimate factfinders in criminal prosecutions, has historically permitted triers of fact to draw on the standards of their community, guided always by limiting instructions on the law. To require a State to structure obscenity proceedings around evidence of a *national* "community standard" would be an exercise in futility.

. . . [T]his case was tried on the theory that the California obscenity statute sought to incorporate the tripartite test of *Memoirs*. This, a "national" standard of First Amendment protection enumerated by a plurality of this Court, was correctly regarded at the time of trial as limiting state prosecution under the controlling case law. The jury, however, was explicitly instructed that, in determining whether the "dominant theme of the material as a whole . . . appeals to the prurient interest" and in determining whether the material "goes substantially beyond customary limits of candor and affronts contemporary community standards of decency," it was to apply "contemporary community standards of the State of California."

During the trial, both the prosecution and the defense assumed that the relevant "community standards" in making the factual determination of obscenity were those of the State of California, not some hypothetical standard of the entire United States of America. Defense counsel at trial never objected to the testimony of the State's expert on community standards or to the instructions of the trial judge on "statewide" standards. On appeal to the Appellate Department, Superior Court of California, County of Orange, appellant for the first time contended that application of state, rather than national, standards violated the First and Fourteenth Amendments.

We conclude that neither the State's alleged failure to offer evidence of "national standards," nor the trial court's charge that the jury consider state community standards, were constitutional errors. Nothing in the First Amendment requires that a jury must consider hypothetical and unascertainable "national standards" when attempting to determine whether certain materials are obscene as a matter of fact. . . .

It is neither realistic nor constitutionally sound to read the
First Amendment as requiring that the people of Maine or Mississippi accept public depiction of conduct found tolerable in
Las Vegas, or New York City. . . . People in different States
vary in their tastes and attitudes, and this diversity is not to be
strangled by the absolutism of imposed uniformity. As the Court
made clear in *Mishkin* v. *New York,* . . . the primary concern
with requiring a jury to apply the standard of "the average person, applying contemporary community standards" is to be certain that, so far as material is not aimed at a deviant group, it will
be judged by its impact on an average person, rather than a particularly susceptible or sensitive person—or indeed a totally in-
sensitive one. . . . We hold that the requirement that the jury
evaluate the materials with reference to "contemporary standards of the State of California" serves this protective purpose
and is constitutionally adequate.

IV

The dissenting Justices sound the alarm of repression. But, in
our view, to equate the free and robust exchange of ideas and
political debate with commercial exploitation of obscene material demeans the grand conception of the First Amendment and its
high purposes in the historic struggle for freedom. It is a "misuse of the great guarantees of free speech and free press. . . ."
Breard v. *Alexandria.* . . . The First Amendment protects
works which, taken as a whole, have serious literary, artistic,
political, or scientific value, regardless of whether the government or a majority of the people approve of the ideas these
works represent. "The protection given speech and press was
fashioned to assure unfettered interchange of *ideas* for the
bringing about of political and social changes desired by the people," *Roth* v. *United States* . . . (emphasis added). . . . But
the public portrayal of hard-core sexual conduct for its own
sake, and for the ensuing commercial gain, is a different matter.

There is no evidence, empirical or historical, that the stern
19th century American censorship of public distribution and display of material relating to sex . . . in any way limited or
affected expression of serious literary, artistic, political, or
scentific ideas. On the contrary, it is beyond any question that
the era following Thomas Jefferson to Theodore Roosevelt was
an "extraordinarily vigorous period," not just in economics and
politics, but in *belles lettres* and in "the outlying fields of social

and political philosophies." We do not see the harsh hand of censorship of ideas—good or bad, sound or unsound—and "repression" of political liberty lurking in every state regulation of commercial exploitation of human interest in sex.

Mr. Justice Brennan finds "it is hard to see how state-ordered regimentation of our minds can ever be forestalled." *Paris Adult Theatre I* v. *Slaton.* . . . These doleful anticipations assume that courts cannot distinguish commerce in ideas, protected by the First Amendment, from commercial exploitation of obscene material. Moreover, state regulation of hard-core pornography so as to make it unavailable to nonadults, a regulation which Mr. Justice Brennan finds constitutionally permissible, has all the elements of "censorship" for adults; indeed even more rigid enforcement techniques may be called for with such dichotomy of regulation. See *Interstate Circuit, Inc.* v. *Dallas.* . . . [A footnote adds: "[W]e have indicated . . . that because of its strong and abiding interest in youth, a State may regulate the dissemination to juveniles of, and their access to, material objectionable as to them, but which a State clearly could not regulate as to adults. *Ginsberg* v. *New York.* . . ."] One can concede that the "sexual revolution" of recent years may have had useful by-products in striking layers of prudery from a subject long irrationally kept from needed ventilation. But it does not follow that no regulation of patently offensive "hard core" materials is needed or permissible; civilized people do not allow unregulated access to heroin because it is a derivative of medicinal morphine.

In sum, we (a) reaffirm the *Roth* holding that obscene material is not protected by the First Amendment; (b) hold that such material can be regulated by the States, subject to the specific safeguards enunciated above, without a showing that the material is "*utterly* without redeeming social value"; and (c) hold that obscenity is to be determined by applying "contemporary community standards," . . . not "national standards." The judgment of the Appellate Department of the Superior Court, Orange County, California, is vacated and the case remanded to that court for further proceedings not inconsistent with the First Amendment standards established by this opinion. . . .

Vacated and remanded.

Justice William O. Douglas dissenting, asserted that the obscenity test enunciated by the majority

opinion constituted new standards that "we our-
selves [the court] have written into the Constitu-
tion." He wrote:

I

Today we leave open the way for California to send a man to
prison for distributing brochures that advertise books and a
movie under freshly written standards defining obscenity which
until today's decision were never the part of any law.

The Court has worked hard to define obscenity and concededly has failed. In *Roth* v. *United States* . . . it ruled that "[o]bscene material is material which deals with sex in a manner appealing to prurient interest." . . . Obscenity, it was said, was rejected by the First Amendment because it is "utterly without redeeming social importance." . . . The presence of a "prurient interest" was to be determined by "contemporary community standards." . . . That test, it has been said, could not be determined by one standard here and another standard there, *Jacobellis* v. *Ohio,* . . . but "on the basis of a national standard." . . . My Brother Stewart in *Jacobellis* commented that the difficulty of the Court in giving content to obscenity was that it was "faced with the task of trying to define what may be indefinable." . . .

In *Memoirs* v. *Massachusetts,* . . . the *Roth* test was elaborated to read as follows: "[T]hree elements must coalesce: it must be established that (a) the dominant theme of the material taken as a whole appeals to a prurient interest in sex; (b) the material is patently offensive because it affronts contemporary community standards relating to the description or representation of sexual matters; and (c) the material is utterly without redeeming social value."

In *Ginzburg* v. *United States,* . . . a publisher was sent to prison, not for the kind of books and periodicals he sold, but for the manner in which the publications were advertised. . . . The Court said, "Where the purveyor's sole emphasis is on the sexually provocative aspects of his publications, that fact may be decisive in the determination of obscenity." . . . As Mr. Justice Black said in dissent, ". . . Ginzburg . . . is now finally and authoritatively condemned to serve five years in prison for distributing printed matter about sex which neither Ginzburg nor anyone else could possibly have known to be criminal." . . .

A further refinement was added by *Ginsberg* v. *New York,* . . . where the Court held that "it was not irrational for the legislature to find that exposure to material condemned by the statute is harmful to minors."

But even those members of this Court who had created the new and changing standards of "obscenity" could not agree on their application. And so we adopted a *per curiam* treatment of so-called obscene publications that seemed to pass constitutional muster under the several constitutional tests which had been formulated. . . . Some condemn it if its "dominant tendency might be to 'deprave or corrupt' a reader." Others look not to the content of the book but to whether it is advertised " 'to appeal to the erotic interests of customers.' " Some condemn only "hard-core pornography"; but even then a true definition is lacking. It has indeed been said of that definition, "I could never succeed in [defining it] intelligibly," but "I know it when I see it."

Today we would add a new three-pronged test: "(a) whether 'the average person, applying contemporary community standards' would find that the work, taken as a whole, appeals to the prurient interest, . . . (b) whether the work depicts or describes, in a patently offensive way, sexual conduct specifically defined by the applicable state law, and (c) whether the work, taken as a whole, lacks serious literary, artistic, political, or scientific value."

Those are the standards we ourselves have written into the Constitution.* Yet how under these vague tests can we sustain convictions for the sale of an article prior to the time when some court has declared it to be obscene?

---

*Justice Douglas's footnote:

At the conclusion of a two-year study, the U.S. Commission on Obscenity & Pornography determined that the standards we have written interfere with constitutionally protected materials: "Society's attempts to legislate for adults in the area of obscenity have not been successful. Present laws prohibiting the consensual sale or distribution of explicit sexual materials to adults are extremely unsatisfactory in their practical application. The Constitution permits material to be deemed 'obscene' for adults only if, as a whole, it appeals to the 'prurient' interest of the average person, is 'patently offensive' in light of 'community standards,' and lacks 'redeeming social value.' These vague and highly subjective aesthetic, psychological and moral tests do not provide meaningful guidance for law enforcement officials, juries or courts. As a result, law is inconsistently and sometimes erroneously applied and the distinc-

Today the Court retreats from the earlier formulations of the constitutional test and undertakes to make new definitions. . . . The difficulty is that we do not deal with constitutional terms, since "obscenity" is not mentioned in the Constitution or Bill of Rights. And the First Amendment makes no such exception from "the press" which it undertakes to protect nor, as I have said on other occasions, is an exception necessarily implied, for there was no recognized exception to the free press at the time the Bill of Rights was adopted which treated "obscene" publications differently from other types of papers, magazines, and books. So there are no constitutional guidelines for deciding what is and what is not "obscene." The Court is at large because we deal with tastes and standards of literature. What shocks me may be sustenance for my neighbor. What causes one person to boil up in rage over one pamphlet or movie may reflect only his neurosis, not shared by others. We deal here with a regime of censorship which, if adopted, should be done by constitutional amendment after full debate by the people.

Obscenity cases usually generate tremendous emotional outbursts. They have no business being in the courts. If a constitutional amendment authorized censorship, the censor would probably be an administrative agency. Then criminal prosecutions could follow as, if, and when publishers defied the censor and sold their literature. Under that regime a publisher would know when he was on dangerous ground. Under the present regime—whether the old standards or the new ones are used—the criminal law becomes a trap. A brand new test would put a publisher behind bars under a new law improvised by the courts after the publication. That was done in *Ginzburg* and has all the evils of an *ex post facto* law.

My contention is that until a civil proceeding has placed a tract beyond the pale, no criminal prosecution should be sustained. For no more vivid illustration of vague and uncertain laws could be designed than those we have fashioned. As Mr. Justice Harlan has said: "The upshot of all this divergence in viewpoint is that anyone who undertakes to examine the Court's decisions

---

tions made by courts between prohibited and permissible materials often appear indefensible. Errors in the application of the law and uncertainty about its scope also cause interference with the communication of constitutionally protected materials." Report of the Commission on Obscenity and Pornography 53 (1970).

since *Roth* which have held particular material obscene or not obscene would find himself in utter bewilderment." *Interstate Circuit, Inc.* v. *Dallas.* . . .

In any case—certainly when constitutional rights are concerned—we should not allow men to go to prison or be fined when they had no "fair warning" that what they did was criminal conduct.

II

If a specific book, play, paper, or motion picture has in a civil proceeding been condemned as obscene and review of that finding has been completed, and thereafter a person publishes, shows, or displays that particular book or film, then a vague law has been made specific. There would remain the underlying question whether the First Amendment allows an implied exception in the case of obscenity. I do not think it does. . . . But at least a criminal prosecution brought at that juncture would not violate the time-honored void-for-vagueness test.

No such protective procedure has been designed by California in this case. Obscenity—which even we cannot define with precision—is a hodge-podge. To send men to jail for violating standards they cannot understand, construe, and apply is a monstrous thing to do in a Nation dedicated to fair trials and due process.

III

While the right to know is the corollary of the right to speak or publish, no one can be forced by government to listen to disclosure that he finds offensive. . . . There is no "captive audience" problem in these obscenity cases. No one is being compelled to look or to listen. Those who enter newsstands or bookstalls may be offended by what they see. But they are not compelled by the State to frequent those places; and it is only state or governmental action against which the First Amendment, applicable to the States by virtue of the Fourteenth, raises a ban.

The idea that the First Amendment permits government to ban publications that are "offensive" to some people puts an ominous gloss on freedom of the press. That test would make it possible to ban any paper or any journal or magazine in some benighted place. The First Amendment was designed "to invite dispute," to induce "a condition of unrest," to "create dissatisfaction with conditions as they are," and even to stir "people to anger." *Terminiello* v. *Chicago*. . . . The idea that the First Amendment permits punishment for ideas that are "offensive" to the particular judge or jury sitting in judgment is astounding. No greater leveler of speech or literature has ever been designed. To give the power to the censor, as we do today, is to make a sharp and radical break with the traditions of a free society. The First Amendment was not fashioned as a vehicle for dispensing tranquilizers to the people. Its prime function was to keep debate open to "offensive" as well as to "staid" people. The tendency throughout history has been to subdue the individual and to exalt the power of government. The use of the standard "offensive" gives authority to government that cuts the very vitals out of the First Amendment. As is intimated by the Court's opinion, the materials before us may be garbage. But so is much of what is said in political campaigns, in the daily press, on TV, or over the radio. By reason of the First Amendment—and solely because of it—speakers and publishers have not been threatened or subdued because their thoughts and ideas may be "offensive" to some. . . .

If there are to be restraints on what is obscene, then a constitutional amendment should be the way of achieving the end. . . .

We deal with highly emotional, not rational, questions. To many the Song of Solomon is obscene. I do not think we, the judges, were ever given the constitutional power to make definitions of obscenity. If it is to be defined, let the people debate and decide by a constitutional amendment what they want to ban as obscene and what standards they want the legislatures and the courts to apply. . . . Whatever the choice, the courts will have some guidelines. Now we have none except our own predilections.

FCC Upheld in Attack on 'Filthy Words' Broadcast

> *The Supreme Court July 3, 1978 upheld the right of the Federal Communications Commission to proscribe the broadcasting of language that was "indecent" even if not legally "obscene." In a 5–4 ruling in the case of* Federal Communications Commission v. Pacifica Foundation, *the majority opinion held that the ban against prior censorship*

*by the FCC did not preclude the review of com-
pleted broadcasts. Of all forms of communication, the opinion said, broadcasting had the most
limited First Amendment protection. Justice John
Paul Stevens delivered the opinion of the court in
Parts I, II, III and IV-C below and additional
views (Parts IV-A and IV-B) in which Chief Justice Warren E. Burger and Justice William H.
Rehnquist joined. Stevens wrote:*

This case requires that we decide whether the Federal Communications Commission has any power to regulate a radio
broadcast that is indecent but not obscene.

A satiric humorist named George Carlin recorded a 12-minute
monologue entitled "Filthy Words" before a live audience in a
California theater. He began by referring to his thoughts about
"the words you couldn't say on the public, ah, airwaves, um,
the ones you definitely wouldn't say, ever." He proceeded to list
those words and repeat them over and over again in a variety of
colloquialisms. The transcript of the recording, which is append-
ed to this opinion, indicates frequent laughter from the audience.

At about 2 o'clock in the afternoon on Tuesday, October 30,
1973, a New York radio station owned by respondent, Pacifica
Foundation, broadcast the "Filthy Words" monologue. A few
weeks later a man, who stated that he had heard the broadcast
while driving with his young son, wrote a letter complaining to
the Commission. . . .

The complaint was forwarded to the station for comment. In
its response, Pacifica explained that the monologue had been
played during a program about contemporary society's attitude
toward language and that immediately before its broadcast listeners had been advised that it included "sensitive language
which might be regarded as offensive to some." Pacifica characterized George Carlin as "a significant social satirist" who "like
[Mark] Twain and [Mort] Sahl before him, examines the language of ordinary people. . . . Carlin is not mouthing obscenities, he is merely using words to satirize as harmless and essentially silly our attitudes towards those words." Pacifica stated
that it was not aware of any other complaints about the broadcast.

On February 21, 1975, the Commission issued a Declaratory

Order granting the complaint and holding that Pacifica "could have been the subject of administrative sanctions." . . . The Commission did not impose formal sanctions, but it did state that the order would be "associated with the station's license file, and in the event that subsequent complaints are received, the Commission will then decide whether it should utilize any of the available sanctions it has been granted by Congress." [A footnote said that the FCC noted: "Congress has specifically empowered the FCC to (1) revoke a station's license (2) issue a cease and desit order, or (3) impose a monetary forfeiture for a violation of Section 1464, 47 U. S. C. 312 (a), 312 (b), 503 (b)(1)(E). The FCC can also (4) deny license renewal or (5) grant a short term renewal, 47 U.S.C. 307, 308." . . .]

In its Memorandum Opinion the Commission stated that it intended to "clarify the standards which will be utilized in considering" the growing number of complaints about indecent speech on the airwaves. . . . Advancing several reasons for treating broadcast speech differently from other forms of expression,* the Commission found a power to regulate indecent broadcasting in two statutes: 18 U.S.C.§ 1464, which forbids the use of "any obscene, indecent, or profane language by means of radio communications," and 47 U.S.C. § 303 (g), which requires the Commission to "encourage the larger and more effective use of radio in the public interest."

The Commission characterized the language used in the Carlin monologue as "patently offensive," though not necessarily obscene, and expressed the opinion that it should be regulated by principles analogous to those found in the law of nuisance where the "law generally speaks to *channeling* behavior more than actually prohibiting it. . . . [T]he concept of 'indecent' is intimately connected with the exposure of children to language that describes, in terms patently offensive as measured by contem-

---

*"Broadcasting requires special treatment because of four important considerations: (1) children have access to radios and in many cases are unsupervised by parents; (2) radio receivers are in the home, a place where people's privacy interest is entitled to extra deference, see *Rowan* v. *Post Office Dept.* . . . (1970); (3) unconsenting adults may tune in a station without any warning that offensive language is being or will be broadcast; and (4) there is a scarcity of spectrum space, the use of which the government must therefore license in the public interest. Of special concern to the Commission as well as parents is the first point regarding the use of radio by children." . . .

porary community standards for the broadcast medium, sexual or excretory activities and organs, at times of the day when there is a reasonable risk that children may be in the audience." . . .

Applying these considerations to the language used in the monologue as broadcast by repondent, the Commission concluded that certain words depicted sexual and excretory activities in a patently offensive manner, noted that they "were broadcast at a time when children were undoubtedly in the audience (*i.e.*, in the early afternoon)," and that the prerecorded language, with these offensive words "repeated over and over," was "deliberately broadcast." . . . In summary, the Commission stated: "We therefore hold that the language as broadcast was indecent and prohibited by 18 U.S.C. 1464." [A footnote said that FCC Commissioner Glen O. Robinson, joined by Commissioner Benjamin L. Hooks, filed a concurring statement expressing the opinion that "we can regulate offensive speech to the extent it constitutes a public nuisance. . . . The governing idea is that 'indecency' is not an inherent attribute of words themselves; it is rather a matter of context and conduct. . . . If I were called on to do so, I would find that Carlin's monologue, if it were broadcast at an appropriate hour and accompanied by suitable warning, was distinguished by sufficient literary value to avoid being 'indecent' within the meaning of the statute." . . .]

After the order issued, the Commission was asked to clarify its opinion by ruling that the broadcast of indecent words as part of a live newscast would not be prohibited. The Commission issued another opinion in which it pointed out that it "never intended to place an absolute prohibition on the broadcast of this type of language, but rather sought to channel it to times of day when children most likely would not be exposed to it." . . . The Commission noted that its "declaratory order was issued in a specific factual context," and declined to comment on various hypothetical situations presented by the petition. [According to a footnote, the Commission did, however, comment that: " '[I]n some cases, public events likely to produce offensive speech are covered live, and there is no opportunity for journalistic edition.' Under these circumstances we believe that it would be inequitable for us to hold a licensee responsible for indecent language. . . . We trust that under such circumstances a licensee will exercise judgment, responsibility, and sensitivity to the community's needs, interests and tastes." . . .] . . .

The United States Court of Appeals for the District of Columbia reversed, with each of the three judges on the panel writing separately. . . . Judge [Edward Allen] Tamm concluded that the order represented censorship and was expressly prohibited by § 326 of the Communications Act. Alternatively, Judge Tamm read the Commission opinion as the functional equivalent of a rule and concluded that it was "overbroad." . . . Chief Judge [David L.] Bazelon's concurrence rested on the Constitution. He was persuaded that § 326's prohibition against censorship is inapplicable to broadcasts forbidden by § 1464. However, he concluded that § 1464 must be narrowly construed to cover only language that is obscene or otherwise unprotected by the First Amendment. . . . Judge [Harold] Leventhal, in dissent, stated that the only issue was whether the Commission could regulate the language *"as broadcast."* . . . Emphasizing the interest in protecting children, not only from exposure to indecent language, but also from exposure to the idea that such language has official approval, . . . he concluded that the Commission had correctly condemned the daytime broadcast as indecent. . . .

I

The general statements in the Commission's memorandum opinion do not change the character of its order. Its action was an adjudication under 5 U.S.C. § 554 (e) (1976 ed.); it did not purport to engage in formal rulemaking or in the promulgation of any regulations. The order "was issued in a special factual context"; questions concerning possible action in other contexts were expressly reserved for the future. The specific holding was carefully confined to the monologue "as broadcast."

"This Court . . . reviews judgments, not statements in opinions." *Black* v. *Cutter Laboratories.* . . . That admonition has special force when the statements raise constitutional questions, for it is our settled practice to avoid the unnecessary decision of such issues. . . . However appropriate it may be for an administrative agency to write broadly in an adjudicatory proceeding, federal courts have never been empowered to issue advisory opinions. . . . Accordingly, the focus of our review must be on the Commission's determination that the Carlin monologue was indecent as broadcast.

II

The relevant statutory questions are whether the Commission's action is forbidden "censorship" within the meaning of 47 U.S.C. § 326 and whether speech that concededly is not obscene may be restricted as "indecent" under the authority of 18 U.S.C. § 1464. . . .

Section 29 of the Radio Act of 1927 provided: "Nothing in this Act shall be understood or construed to give the licensing authority the power of censorship over the radio communications or signals transmitted by any radio station, and no regulation or condition shall be promulgated or fixed by the licensing authority which shall interfere with the right of free speech by means of radio communications. No person within the jurisdiction of the United States shall utter any obscene, indecent, or profane language by means of radio communication." . . .

The prohibition against censorship unequivocally denies the Commission any power to edit proposed broadcasts in advance and to excise material considered inappropriate for the airwaves. The prohibition, however, has never been construed to deny the Commission the power to review the content of completed broadcasts in the performance of its regulatory duties.

During the period between the original enactment of the provision in 1927 and its re-enactment in the Communications Act of 1934, the courts and the Federal Radio Commission held that the section deprived the Commission of the power to subject "broadcasting matter to scrutiny prior to its release," but they concluded that the Commission's "undoubted right" to take note of past program content when considering a licensee's renewal application "is not censorship." [A footnote referred to the case of *Trinity Methodist Church, South* v. *Federal Radio Commission* (1933). The station was controlled by a minister whose broadcasts contained frequent references to "pimps" and "prostitutes" as well as bitter attacks on the Roman Catholic Church. The Commission refused to renew the license, citing the nature of the broadcasts. The Court of Appeals affirmed, concluding that First Amendment concerns did not prevent the Commission from regulating broadcasts that "offend the religious suceptibilities of thousands . . . or offend youth and innocence by the free use of words suggestive of sexual immorality." The court recognized that the licensee had a right to broadcast this material free of prior restraint, but "this does not mean that the government, through agencies established by Congress, may not refuse a renewal of license to one who has abused it.'']

Not only did the Federal Radio Commission so construe the statute prior to 1934; its successor, the Federal Communications Commission, has consistently interpreted the provision in the same way ever since. . . . And, until this case, the Court of Appeals for the District of Columbia has consistently agreed with this construction. . . .

Entirely apart from the fact that the subsequent review of program content is not the sort of censorship at which the statute was directed, its history makes it perfectly clear that it was not intended to limit the Commission's power to regulate the broadcast of obscene, indecent, or profane language. A single section of the 1927 Act is the source of both the anticensorship provision and the Commission's authority to impose sanctions for the broadcast of indecent or obscene language. Quite plainly, Congress intended to give meaning to both provisions. Respect for that intent requires that the censorship language be read as inapplicable to the prohibition on broadcasting obscene, indecent, or profane language.

There is nothing in the legislative history to contradict this conclusion. . . . In 1934, the anticensorship provision and the prohibition against indecent broadcasts were re-enacted in the same section, just as in the 1927 Act. In 1948, when the Criminal Code was revised to include provisions that had previously been located in other titles of the United States Code, the prohibition against obscene, indecent, and profane broadcasts was removed from the Communications Act and re-enacted as § 1464 of Title 18. . . . That rearrangement of the Code cannot reasonably be interpreted as having been intended to change the meaning of the anticensorship provision. . . .

We conclude, therefore, that § 326 does not limit the Commission's authority to impose sanctions on licensees who engage in obscene, indecent, or profane broadcasting

III

The only other statutory question presented by this case is whether the afternoon broadcast of the "Filthy Words" monologue was indecent within the meaning of § 1464. . . .

The Commission identified several words that referred to excretory or sexual activities or organs, stated that the repetitive, deliberate use of those words in an afternoon broadcast when children are in the audience was patently offensive, and held that the broadcast was indecent. Pacifica takes issue with the Commission's definition of indecency, but does not dispute the Commission's preliminary determination that each of the components of its definition was present. Specifically, Pacifica does not quarrel with the conclusion that this afternoon broadcast was patently offensive. Pacifica's claim that the broadcast was not indecent within the meaning of the statute rests entirely on the absence of prurient appeal.

The plain language of the statute does not support Pacifica's argument. The words "obscene, indecent, or profane" are written in the disjunctive, implying that each has a separate meaning. Prurient appeal is an element of the obscene, but the normal definition of "indecent" merely refers to nonconformance with accepted standards of morality.

Pacifica argues, however, that this Court has construed the term "indecent" in related statutes to mean "obscene," as that term was defined in *Miller* v. *California.* . . . Pacifica relies most heavily on the construction this Court gave to 18 U.S.C. § 1461 in *Hamling* v. *United States.* . . . *Hamling* rejected a vagueness attack on § 1461, which forbids the mailing of "obscene, lewd, lascivious, indecent, filthy or vile" material. In holding that the statute's coverage is limited to obscenity, the Court followed the lead of Mr. Justice Harlan in *Manual Enterprises, Inc.* v. *Day.* . . . In that case, Mr. Justice Harlan recognized that § 1461 contained a variety of words with many shades of meaning. Nonetheless, he thought that the phrase "obscene, lewd, lascivious, indecent, filthy or vile," taken as a whole, was clearly limited to the obscene, a reading well-grounded in prior judicial constructions: "the statute since its inception has always been taken as aimed at obnoxiously debasing portrayals of sex." . . . In *Hamling* the Court agreed with Mr. Justice Harlan that § 1461 was meant only to regulate obscenity in the mails; by reading into it the limits set by *Miller* v. *California,* . . . the Court adopted a construction which assured the statute's constitutionality.

The reasons supporting *Hamling*'s construction of § 1461 do not apply to § 1464. Although the history of the former revealed a primary concern with the prurient, the Commission has long interpreted § 1464 as encompassing more than the obscene. The former statute deals primarily with printed matter enclosed in sealed envelopes mailed from one individual to another; the latter deals with the content of public broadcasts. It is unrealistic to assume that Congress intended to impose precisely the same limitations on the dissemination of patently offensive matter by such different means.

Because neither our prior decisions nor the language or history of § 1464 supports the conclusion that prurient appeal is an essential component of indecent language, we reject Pacifica's construction of the statute. When that construction is put to one side, there is no basis for disagreeing with the Commission's conclusion that indecent language was used in this broadcast.

IV

Pacifica makes two constitutional attacks on the Commission's order. First, it argues that the Commission's construction of the statutory language broadly encompasses so much constitutionally protected speech that reversal is required even if Pacifica's broadcast of the "Filthy Words" monologue is not itself protected by the First Amendment. Second, Pacifica argues that inasmuch as the recording is not obscene, the Constitution forbids any abridgment of the right to broadcast it on the radio.

A

The first argument fails because our review is limited to the question whether the Commission has the authority to proscribe this particular broadcast. As the Commission itself emphasized, its order was "issued in a specific factual context." . . . That approach is appropriate for courts as well as the Commission when regulation of indecency is at stake, for indecency is largely a function of context—it cannot be adequately judged in the abstract.

The approach is also consistent with *Red Lion Broadcasting Co., Inc.* v. *FCC*. . . . In that case the Court rejected an argument that the Commission's regulations defining the fairness doctrine were so vague that they would inevitably abridge the broadcasters' freedom of speech. . . .

It is true that the Commission's order may lead some broadcasters to censor themselves. At most, however, the Commission's definition of indecency will deter only the broadcasting of patently offensive references to excretory and sexual organs and activities. [According to a footnote: A requirement that indecent language be avoided will have its primary effect on the form, rather than the content, of serious communication. There are few, if any, thoughts that cannot be expressed by the use of less

offensive language.] While some of these references may be
protected, they surely lie at the periphery of First Amendment
concern. . . . The danger dismissed so summarily in *Red Lion*,
in contrast, was that broadcasters would respond to the vagueness of the regulations by refusing to present programs dealing
with important social and political controversies. Invalidating
any rule on the basis of its hypothetical application to situations
not before the Court is "strong medicine" to be applied "spar-
ingly and only as a last resort." *Broadrick* v. *Oklahoma.* . . . We decline to administer that medicine to preserve the vigor of patently offensive sexual and excretory
speech.

B

When the issue is narrowed to the facts of this case, the question is whether the First Amendment denies government any
power to restrict the public broadcast of indecent language in
any circumstances.* For if the government has any such power,
this was an appropriate occasion for its exercise.

The words of the Carlin monologue are unquestionably
"speech" within the meaning of the First Amendment. It is
equally clear that the Commission's objections to the broadcast
were based in part on its content. The order must therefore fall
if, as Pacifica argues, the First Amendment prohibits all governmental regulation that depends on the content of speech. Our
past cases demonstrate, however, that no such absolute rule is
mandated by the Constitution.

The classic exposition of the proposition that both the content
and the context of speech are critical elements of First Amendment analysis is Mr. Justice Holmes' statement for the Court in
Schenk v. *United States:* "We admit that in many places and in
ordinary times the defendants in saying all that was said in the

---

*Pacifica's position would of course deprive the Commission of any power to
regulate erotic telecasts unless they were obscene under *Miller* v. *California.* . . . Anything that could be sold at a newstand for private examination could be publicly displayed on television. We are assured by Pacifica that
the free play of market forces will discourage indecent programming. "Smut
may," as Judge Leventhal put it, "drive itself from the market and confound
Gresham," . . .; the prosperity of those who traffic in pornographic literature
and films would appear to justify his skepticism.

circular would have been within their constitutional rights. But the character of every act depends upon the circumstances in which it is done. . . . The most stringent protection of free speech would not protect a man in falsely shouting fire in a theatre and causing a panic. It does not even protect a man from an injunction against uttering words that may have all the effect of force. . . . The question in every case is whether the words used are used in such circumstances and are of such a nature as to create a clear and present danger that they will bring about the substantive evils that Congress has a right to prevent." . . . Other distinctions based on content have been approved in the years since *Schenck* . . . Obscenity may be wholly prohibited. *Miller* v. *California.* . . .

The question in this case is whether a broadcast of patently offensive words dealing with sex and excretion may be regulated because of its content. Obscene materials have been denied the protection of the First Amendment because their content is so offensive to contemporary moral standards. *Roth* v. *United States.* . . . But the fact that society may find speech offensive is not a sufficient reason for suppressing it. Indeed, if it is the speaker's opinion that gives offense, that consequence is a reason for according it constitutional protection. For it is a central tenet of the First Amendment that the government must remain neutral in the marketplace of ideas. If there were any reason to believe that the Commission's characterization of the Carlin monologue as offensive could be traced to its political content— or even to the fact that it satirized contemporary attitudes about four letter words†—First Amendment protection might be required. But that is simply not this case. These words offend for the same reasons that obscenity offends. [A footnote quoted the FCC as saying: "Obnoxious, gutter language describing these matters has the effect of debasing and brutalizing human beings by reducing them to their mere bodily functions. . . ." . . .

---

†The monologue does present a point of view; it attempts to show that the words it uses are "harmless" and that our attitudes toward them are "essentially silly." . . . The Commission objects, not to this point of view, but to the way in which it is expressed. The belief that these words are harmless does not necessarily confer a First Amendment privilege to use them while proselytizing, just as the conviction that obscenity is harmless does not license one to communicate that conviction by the indiscriminate distribution of an obscene leaflet.

Our society has a tradition of performing certain bodily functions in private, and of severely limiting the public exposure or discussion of such matters. Verbal or physical acts exposing those intimacies are offensive irrespective of any message that may accompany the exposure.] Their place in the hierarchy of First Amendment values was aptly sketched by Mr. Justice Murphy when he said, "such utterances are no essential part of any exposition of ideas, and are of such slight social value as a step to truth that any benefit that may be derived from them is clearly outweighed by the social interest in order and morality." *Chaplinsky* v. *New Hampshire*. . . .

Although these words ordinarily lack literary, political, or scientific value, they are not entirely outside the protection of the First Amendment. Some uses of even the most offensive words are unquestionably protected. See, *e. g., Hess* v. *Indiana*. . . . Indeed, we may assume, *arguendo*, that this monologue would be protected in other contexts. Nonetheless, the constitutional protection accorded to a communication containing such patently offensive sexual and excretory language need not be the same in every context. It is a characteristic of speech such as this that both its capacity to offend and its "social value," to use Mr. Justice Murphy's term, vary with the circumstances. Words that are commonplace in one setting are shocking in another. To paraphrase Mr. Justice Harlan, one occasion's lyric is another's vulgarity. Cf. *Cohen* v. *California*, 403 U. S. 15, 25 §

---

§The importance of context is illustrated by the *Cohen* case. That case arose when Paul Cohen entered a Los Angeles courthouse wearing a jacket emblazoned with the words "Fuck the Draft." After entering the courtroom, he took the jacket off and folded it. . . . So far as the evidence showed, no one in the courthouse was offended by his jacket. Nonetheless, when he left the courtroom, Cohen was arrested, convicted of disturbing the peace, and sentenced to 30 days in prison. In holding that criminal sanctions could not be imposed on Cohen for his political statement in a public place, the Court rejected the argument that his speech would offend unwilling viewers; it noted that "there was no evidence that persons powerless to avoid [his] conduct did in fact object to it." . . . In contrast, in this case the Commission was responding to a listener's strenuous complaint, and Pacifica does not question its determination that this afternoon broadcast was likely to offend listeners. It should be noted that the Commission imposed a far more moderate penalty on Pacifica than the state court imposed on Cohen. Even the strongest civil penalty at the Commission's command does not include criminal prosecution. . . .

In this case it is undisputed that the content of Pacifica's broadcast was "vulgar," "offensive," and "shocking." Because content of that character is not entitled to absolute constitutional protection under all circumstances, we must consider its context in order to determine whether the Commission's action was constitutionally permissible.

C

We have long recognized that each medium of expression presents special First Amendment problems. *Joseph Burstyn, Inc.* v. *Wilson* . . . And of all forms of communication, it is broadcasting that has received the most limited First Amendment protection. Thus, although other speakers cannot be licensed except under laws that carefully define and narrow official discretion, a broadcaster may be deprived of his license and his forum if the Commission decides that such an action would serve "the public interest, convenience, and necessity." Similarly, although the First Amendment protects newspaper publishers from being required to print the replies of those whom they criticize, *Miami Herald Publishing Co.* v. *Tornillo,* . . . it affords no such protection to broadcasters; on the contrary, they must give free time to the victims of their criticism. *Red Lion Broadcasting Co., Inc.* v. *FCC.* . . .

The reasons for these distinctions are complex, but two have relevance to the present case. First, the broadcast media have established a uniquely pervasive presence in the lives of all Americans. Patently offensive, indecent material presented over the airwaves confronts the citizen, not only in public, but also in the privacy of the home, where the individual's right to be let alone plainly outweighs the First Amendment rights of an intruder. *Rowan* v. *Post Office Department* . . . Because the broadcast audience is constantly tuning in and out, prior warnings cannot completely protect the listener or viewer from unexpected program content. To say that one may avoid further offense by turning off the radio when he hears indecent language is like saying that the remedy for an assault is to run away after the first blow. One may hang up on an indecent phone call, but that option does not give the caller a constitutional immunity or avoid a harm that has already taken place.

Second, broadcasting is uniquely accessible to children, even those too young to read. Although Cohen's written message might have been incomprehensible to a first grader, Pacifica's broadcast could have enlarged a child's vocabulary in an instant. Other forms of offensive expression may be withheld from the young without restricting the expression at its source. Bookstores and motion picture theaters, for example, may be prohibited from making indecent material available to children. We held in *Ginsberg* v. *New York* . . . that the government's interest in the "well being of its youth" and in supporting "parents' claim to authority in their own household" justified the regulation of otherwise protected expression. . . . [A footnote says: The Commission's action does not by any means reduce adults to hearing only what is fit for children. . . . Adults who feel the need may purchase tapes and records or go to theatres and nightclubs to hear these words. In fact, the Commission has not unequivocally closed even broadcasting to speech of this sort; whether broadcast audiences in the late evening contain so few children that playing this monologue would be permissible is an issue neither the Commission nor this Court has decided.] The ease with which children may obtain access to broadcast material, coupled with the concerns recognized in *Ginsberg*, amply justify special treatment of indecent broadcasting.

It is appropriate, in conclusion, to emphasize the narrowness of our holding. This case does not involve a two-way radio conversation between a cab driver and a dispatcher, or a telecast of an Elizabethan comedy. We have not decided that an occasional expletive in either setting would justify any sanction or, indeed, that this broadcast would justify a criminal prosecution. The Commission's decision rested entirely on a nuisance rationale under which context is all-important. The concept requires consideration of a host of variables. The time of day was emphasized by the Commission. The content of the program in which the language is used will also affect the composition of the audience, and differences between radio, television, and perhaps closed-circuit transmissions, may also be relevant. As Mr. Justice Sutherland wrote, a "nuisance may be merely a right thing in the wrong place—like a pig in the parlor instead of the barnyard." *Euclid* v. *Ambler Realty Co.* . . . We simply hold that when the Commission finds that a pig has entered the parlor, the exercise of its regulatory power does not depend on proof that the pig is obscene.

The judgment of the Court of Appeals is reversed.

APPENDIX

[A verbatim transcript of "Filthy Words," prepared by the FCC, was provided as an appendix to Stevens' opinion. Excerpts of the transcript follow to indicate the effects—literary, satirical, humorous, offensive—the George Carlin monologue was said to produce]

" . . . I was thinking about . . . the cuss words and the words that you can't say, that you're not supposed to say all the time. . . . Some guys like to record your words and sell them back to you if they can, (laughter) listen in on the telephone, write down what words you say. A guy who used to be in Washington knew that his phone was tapped, used to answer, Fuck Hoover, yes, go ahead. (laughter) Okay, I was thinking one night about the words you couldn't say on the public, ah, airwaves, um, the ones you definitely wouldn't say, ever cause I heard a lady say bitch one night on television, and it was cool like she was talking about, you know, ah, well, the bitch is the first one to notice that in the litter Johnie right (murmur). Right. And, uh, bastard you can say, and hell and damn so I have to figure out which ones you couldn't and ever and it came down to seven but the list is open to amendment, and in fact, has been changed, uh, by now . . . . The original seven words were, shit, piss, fuck, cunt, cocksucker, motherfucker, and tits. Those are the ones that will curve your spine, grow hair on your hands and (laughter) maybe, even bring us, God help us, peace without honor (laughter) um, and a bourbon. (laughter) . . .

" . . . Now the word shit is okay for the man. At work you can say it like crazy. Mostly figuratively, Get that shit out of here, will ya? I don't want to see that shit anymore. I can't *cut* that shit, buddy. I've had that shit up to here. I think you're full of shit myself. (laughter) He don't know shit from Shinola. (laughter) you know that? (laughter) Always wondered how the Shinola people felt about that (laughter) Hi, I'm the new man from Shinola. (laughter) . . . Boy, I don't know whether to shit or wind my watch. (laughter) Guess, I'll shit on my watch. (laughter) Oh, *the* shit is going to hit *de* fan. (laughter) Built like a brick shit-house. (laughter) Up, he's up shit's creek. (laughter) . . . Hot shit, holy shit, tough shit, eat shit, (laughter) shit-eating grin. Uh, whoever thought of that was ill. (murmur laughter) He had a shit-eating grin! . . . Shit on a stick. (laughter) Shit in a handbag. I always like that. He ain't worth shit in a handbag. (laughter) . . .

"The big one, the word fuck that's the one that hangs them up the most. Cause in a lot of cases that's the very act that hangs them up the most. So, it's natural that the word would, uh, have the same effect. It's a great word, fuck, nice word, easy word, cute word, kind of. Easy word to say. One syllable, short u. (laughter) Fuck. (Murmur) You know, it's easy. Starts with a nice soft sound fuh ends with a *kuh*. Right? (laughter) A little something for everyone. Fuck (laughter) Good word. Kind of a proud word, too. Who are you? I am *FUCK*. (laughter) . . . It's an interesting word too, cause it's got a double kind of a life— personality—dual, you know, whatever the right phrase is. It leads a double life, the word fuck. First of all, it means, some- times, most of the time, fuck. What does it mean? It means to make love. Right? We're going to make love, yeh, we're going to fuck, yeh, we're going to fuck, yeh, we're going to make love. (laughter) . . . Right? And it also means the beginning of life, it's the act that begins life, so there's the word hanging around with words like love, and life, and yet on the other hand, it's also a word that we really use to hurt each other with, man. It's a heavy. It's one that you save toward the end of the argument. (laughter) Right? (laughter) You finally can't make out. Oh, fuck you man. I said, fuck you. (laughter, murmur) Stupid fuck. (laughter) Fuck you and everybody that looks like you. (laugh- ter) man. It would be nice to change the movies that we already have and substitute the word fuck for the word kill, wherever we could, and some of those movie cliches would change a little bit. Madfuckers still on the loose. Stop me before I fuck again. Fuck the ump, fuck the ump, fuck the ump, fuck the ump, fuck the ump. . . .

"And two-way words. Ah, ass is okay providing you're riding into town on a religious feast day. (laughter) You can't say, up your *ass*. (laughter) You can say, stuff it! (murmur) There are certain things you can say its weird but you can just come so close. Before I cut, I, uh, want to, ah, thank you for listening to my words, man, fellow, uh, space travelers. Thank you man for tonight and thank you also. (clapping, whistling)"

> *Justice Lewis F. Powell Jr., concurring, joined in Parts I, II, III and IV(C) of Stevens' opinion. In an opinion in which Justice Harry A. Blackmun joined, Powell wrote:*

I also agree with much that is said in Part IV of Mr. Justice Stevens' opinion, and with its conclusion that the Commission's holding in this case does not violate the First Amendment. Because I do not subscribe to all that is said in Part IV, however, I state my views separately.

I

It is conceded that the monologue at issue here is not obscene in the constitutional sense. . . . Some of the words used have been held protected by the First Amendment in other cases and contexts. . . . I do not think Carlin, consistently with the First Amendment, could be punished for delivering the same monologue to a live audience composed of adults who, knowing what to expect, chose to attend his performance. . . . And I would assume that an adult could not constitutionally be prohibited from purchasing a recording or transcript of the monologue and playing or reading it in the privacy of his own home. . . .

But it also is true that the language employed is, to most people, vulgar and offensive. It was chosen specifically for this quality, and it was repeated over and over as a sort of verbal shock treatment. The Commission did not err in characterizing the narrow category of language used here as "patently offensive" to most people regardless of age.

The issue, however, is whether the Commission may impose civil sanctions on a licensee radio station for broadcasting the monologue at two o'clock in the afternoon. The Commission's primary concern was to prevent the broadcast from reaching the ears of unsupervised children who were likely to be in the audience at that hour. In essence, the Commission sought to "channel" the monologue to hours when the fewest unsupervised children would be exposed to it. . . . In my view, this consideration provides strong support for the Commission's holding.

The Court has recognized society's right to "adopt more stringent controls on communicative materials available to youths than on those available to adults." *Erznoznik* v. *City of Jacksonville*. . . . The Commission properly held that the speech from which society may attempt to shield its children is not limited to that which appeals to the youthful prurient interest. The language involved in this case is as potentially degrading and harmful to children as representations of many erotic acts.

In most instances, the dissemination of this kind of speech to children may be limited without also limiting willing adults' access to it. Sellers of printed and recorded matter and exhibitors of motion pictures and live performances may be required to shut their doors to children, but such a requirement has no effect on adults' access. . . . The difficulty is that such a physical separation of the audience cannot be accomplished in the broadcast media. During most of the broadcast hours, both adults and unsupervised children are likely to be in the broadcast audience, and the broadcaster cannot reach willing adults without also reaching children. This, as the Court emphasizes, is one of the distinctions between the broadcast and other media to which we often have adverted as justifying a different treatment of the broadcast media for First Amendment purposes. . . . In my view, the Commission was entitled to give substantial weight to this difference in reaching its decision in this case.

A second difference, not without relevance, is that broadcasting—unlike most other forms of communication—comes directly into the home, the one place where people ordinarily have the right not to be assaulted by uninvited and offensive sights and sounds. *Erznoznik* v. *City of Jacksonville* . . . (1975); *Cohen* v. *California* . . . (1971); *Rowen* v. *Post Office Dept.* . . . (1970). Although the First Amendment may require unwilling adults to absorb the first blow of offensive but protected speech when they are in public before they turn away, . . . a different order of values obtains in the home. "That we are often 'captives' outside the sanctuary of the home and subject to objectionable speech and other sound does not mean we must be captives everywhere." *Rowan* v. *Post Office Dept.* . . . The Commission also was entitled to give this factor appropriate weight in the circumstances of the instant case. This is not to say, however, that the Commission has an unrestricted license to decide what speech, protected in other media, may be banned from the airwaves in order to protect unwilling adults from momentary exposure to it in their homes. Making the sensitive judgments required in these cases is not easy. But this responsibility has been reposed initially in the Commission, and its judgment is entitled to respect.

It is argued that despite society's right to protect its children from this kind of speech, and despite everyone's interest in not being assaulted by offensive speech in the home, the Commission's holding in this case is impermissible because it prevents willing adults from listening to Carlin's monologue over the radio in the early afternoon hours. It is said that this ruling will have the effect of "reduc[ing] the adult population . . . to [hearing] only what is fit for children." *Butler* v. *Michigan*. . . . This argument is not without force. The Commission certainly should consider it as it develops standards in this area. But it is not sufficiently strong to leave the Commission powerless to act in circumstances such as those in this case.

The Commission's holding does not prevent willing adults from purchasing Carlin's record, from attending his performances, or, indeed, from reading the transcript reprinted as an appendix to the Court's opinion. On its face, it does not prevent respondent from broadcasting the monologue during late evening hours when fewer children are likely to be in the audience, nor from broadcasting discussions of the contemporary use of language at any time during the day. The Commission's holding, and certainly the Court's holding today, does not speak to cases involving the isolated use of a potentially offensive word in the course of a radio broadcast, as distinguished from the verbal shock treatment administered by respondent here. In short, I agree that on the facts of this case, the Commission's order did not violate respondent's First Amendment rights.

II

As the foregoing demonstrates, my views are generally in accord with what is said in Part IV(C) of Mr. Justice Stevens' opinion. . . . I therefore join that portion of his opinion. I do not join Part IV(B), however, because I do not subscribe to the theory that the Justices of this Court are free generally to decide on the basis of its content which speech protected by the First Amendment is most "valuable" and hence deserving of the most protection, and which is less "valuable" and hence deserving of less protection. . . . In my view, the result in this case does not turn on whether Carlin's monologue, viewed as a whole, or the words that comprise it, have more or less "value" than a candidates's campaign speech. This is a judgment for each person to make, not one for the judges to impose upon him.

The result turns instead on the unique characteristics of the broadcast media, combined with society's right to protect its children from speech generally agreed to be inappropriate for their years, and with the interest of unwilling adults in not being assaulted by such offensive speech in their homes. Moreover, I doubt whether today's decision will prevent any adult who wishes to receive Carlin's message in Carlin's own words from doing so, and from making for himself a value judgment as to the merit of the message and words. . . . These are the grounds upon which I join the judgment of the Court as to Part IV.

> *Justice William J. Brennan, dissenting, charged that the majority misapplied fundamental First Amendment principles, sought "to impose its notion of propriety on the whole of the American people" and even refused "to follow its own [previous] pronouncements." In an opinion in which Justice Thurgood Marshall joined, Brennan wrote:*

I

For the second time in two years, see *Young* v. *American Mini Theatres* . . . (1976), the Court refuses to embrace the notion, completely antithetical to basic First Amendment values, that the degree of protection the First Amendment affords protected speech varies with the social value ascribed to that speech by five Members of this Court. . . . Moreover, as do all parties, all Members of the Court agree that the Carlin monologue aired by Station WBAI does not fall within one of the categories of speech, such as "fighting words," . . . or obscenity, . . . that is totally without First Amendment protection. This conclusion, of course, is compelled by our cases expressly holding that communications containing some of the words found condemnable here are fully protected by the First Amendment in other contexts. See *Eaton* v. *City of Tulsa* . . . (1974); *Papish* v. *University of Missouri Curators* . . . (1973); *Brown* v. *Oklahoma* . . . (1972); *Lewis* v. *New Orleans* . . . (1972); *Rosenfeld* v. *New Jersey* . . . (1972); *Cohen* v. *California* . . . (1971). Yet despite the Court's refusal to create a sliding scale of First Amendment protection calibrated to this Court's perception of the worth of a communication's content, and despite our unanimous agreement that the Carlin monologue is protected speech, a majority of the Court nevertheless finds that, on the facts of this case, the FCC is not constitutionally barred from imposing sanctions on Pacifica for its airing of the Carlin monologue. This majority apparently believes that the FCC's disapproval of Pacifica's afternoon broadcast of Carlin's "Dirty Words'" recording is a permissable time, place, and manner regulation. Both the opinion of my Brother Stevens and the opinion of my Brother Powell rely principally on two factors in reaching this conclusion: (1) the capacity of a radio broadcast to intrude into the unwilling listener's home, and (2) the presence of children in the listening audience. Dispassionate analysis, removed from individual notions as to what is proper and what is not, starkly reveals that these justifications, whether individually or together, simply do not support even the professedly moderate degree of governmental homogenization of radio communications—if, indeed, such homogenization can ever be moderate given the pre-eminent status of the right of free speech in our constitutional scheme—that the Court today permits.

A

Without question, the privacy interests of an individual in his home are substantial and deserving of significant protection. In finding these interests sufficient to justify the content regulation of protected speech, however, the Court commits two errors. First, it misconceives the nature of the privacy interests involved where an individual voluntarily chooses to admit radio communications into his home. Second, it ignores the constitutionally protected interests of both those who wish to transmit and those who desire to receive broadcasts that many might find offensive.

"The ability of government, consonant with the Constitution, to shut off discourse solely to protect others from hearing it is . . . dependent upon a showing that substantial privacy interests are being invaded in an essentially intolerable manner. Any broader view of this authority would effectively empower a majority to silence dissidents simply as a matter of personal predilections." *Cohen v. California.* . . . I believe that an individual's actions in switching on and listening to communications transmitted over the public airways and directed to the public at-large do not implicate fundamental privacy interests, even when engaged in within the home. Instead, because the radio is undeniably a public medium, these actions are more properly viewed as a decision to take part, if only as a listener, in an ongoing public discourse. . . . Although an individual's decision to allow public radio communications into his home undoubtedly does not abrogate all of his privacy interests, the residual privacy interests he retains vis-a-vis the communication he voluntarily admits into his home are surely no greater than those of the people present in the corridor of the Los Angeles courthouse in

Cohen who bore witness to the words "Fuck the Draft" emblazoned across Cohen's jacket. Their privacy interests were held insufficient to justify punishing Cohen for his offensive communication.

Even if an individual who voluntarily opens his home to radio communications retains privacy interests of sufficient moment to justify a ban on protected speech if those interests are "invaded in an essentially intolerable manner," *Cohen* v. *California*, . . . the very fact that those interests are threatened only by a radio broadcast precludes any intolerable invasion of privacy; for unlike other intrusive modes of communication, such as sound trucks, "[t]he radio can be turned off," *Lehman* v. *City of Shaker Heights* . . . (1974)—and with a minimum of effort. As Judge [David L.] Bazelon aptly observed below, "having elected to receive public air waves, the scanner who stumbles onto an offensive program is in the same position as the unsuspected passers-by in *Cohen* and *Erznoznik* [v. *City of Jacksonville*. . . . (1975)]; he can avert his attention by changing channels or turning off the set." . . . Whatever the minimal discomfort suffered by a listener who inadvertently tunes into a program he finds offensive during the brief interval before he can simply extend his arm and switch stations or flick the "off" button, it is surely worth the candle to preserve the broadcaster's right to send, and the right of those interested to receive, a message entitled to full First Amendment protection. . . .

The Court's balance . . . fails to accord proper weight to the interests of listeners who wish to hear broadcasts the FCC deems offensive. It permits majoritarian tastes completely to preclude a protected message from entering the homes of a receptive, unoffended minority. No decision of this Court supports such a result. Where the individuals comprising the offended majority may freely choose to reject the material being offered, we have never found their privacy interests of such moment to warrant the suppression of speech on privacy grounds. . . .

B

Most parents will undoubtedly find understandable as well as commendable the Court's sympathy with the FCC's desire to prevent offensive broadcasts from reaching the ears of unsupervised children. Unfortunately, the facial appeal of this justification for radio censorship masks its constitutional insufficiency. Although the government unquestionably has a special interest in the well-being of children and consequently "can adopt more stringent controls on communicative materials available to youths than on those available to adults," . . . the Court has accounted for this societal interest by adopting a "variable obscenity" standard that permits the prurient appeal of material available to children to be assessed in terms of the sexual interests of minors. . . . [W]e have made it abundantly clear that "under any test of obscenity as to minors . . . to be obscene 'such expression must be, in some significant way, erotic.' " . . .

Because the Carlin monologue is obviously not an erotic appeal to the purient interests of children, the Court, for the first time, allows the government to prevent minors from gaining access to materials that are not obscene, and are therefore protected, as to them. It thus ignores our recent admonition that "[s]peech that is neither obscene as to youths nor subject to some other legitimate proscription cannot be suppressed solely to protect the young from ideas or images that a legislative body thinks unsuitable for them." . . . The Court's refusal to follow its own pronouncements is especially lamentable since it has the anomalous subsidiary effect, at least in the radio context at issue here, of making completely unavailable to adults material which may not constitutionally be kept even from children. . . .

In concluding that the presence of children in the listening audience provides an adequate basis for the FCC to impose sanctions for Pacifica's broadcast of the Carlin monologue, the opinions of my Brother Powell . . . and my Brother Stevens . . . both stress the time-honored right of a parent to raise his child as he sees fit—a right this Court has consistently been vigilant to protect. See *Wisconsin* v. *Yoder* . . . (1972); *Pierce* v. *Society of Sisters* . . . (1925). Yet this principle supports a result directly contrary to that reached by the Court. *Yoder* and *Pierce* hold that parents, *not* the government, have the right to make certain decisions regarding the upbringing of their children. As surprising as it may be to individual Members of this Court, some parents may actually find Mr. Carlin's unabashed attitude towards the seven "dirty words" healthy, and deem it desirable to expose their children to the manner in which Mr. Carlin defuses the taboo surrounding the words. Such parents may constitute a minority of the American public, but the absence of great numbers willing to exercise the right to raise

their children in this fashion does not alter the right's nature or
its existence. Only the Court's regrettable decision does that.

C

As demonstrated above, neither of the factors relied on by
both the opinion of my Brother Powell and the opinion of my
Brother Stevens—the intrusive nature of radio and the presence
of children in the listening audience—can, when taken on its
terms, support the FCC's disapproval of the Carlin monologue. . . . Taken to their logical extreme, these rationales
would support the cleansing of public radio of any "four-letter
words" whatsoever, regardless of their context. The rationales
could justify the banning from radio of a myriad of literary
works, novels, poems, and plays by the likes of Shakespeare,
Joyce, Hemingway, Ben Jonson, Henry Fielding, Robert Burns,
and Chaucer; they could support the suppression of a good deal
of political speech, such as the Nixon tapes; and they could even
provide the basis for imposing sanctions for the broadcast of
certain portions of the Bible. . . .

II

The absence of any hesitancy in the opinions of my Brothers
Powell and Stevens to approve the FCC's censorship of the Carlin monologue on the basis of two demonstrably inadequate
grounds is a function of their perception that the decision will result in little, if any, curtailment of communicative exchanges
protected by the First Amendment. . . . I find the reasoning by
which my Brethren conclude that the FCC censorship they approve will not significantly infringe on First Amendment values
both disingenuous as to reality and wrong as a matter of
law. . . .

III

. . . The words that the Court and the Commission find so
unpalatable may be the stuff of everyday conversations in some,
if not many, of the innumerable subcultures that comprise this
Nation. Academic research indicates that this is indeed the
case. . . . As one researcher concluded, "[w]ords generally
considered obscene like 'bullshit' and 'fuck' are considered neither obscene nor derogatory in the [black] vernacular except in
particular contextual situations and when used with certain into-

nations." C. Bins, "Toward an Ethnography of Contemporary African American Oral Poetry," Language and Linguistics Working Papers No. 5, at 82 (Georgetown University Press 1972). Cf. *Keefe* v. *Geanakos* . . . (CA1 1969) (finding the use of the word "motherfucker" commonplace among young radicals and protestors).

Today's decision will thus have its greatest impact on broadcasters desiring to reach, and listening audiences comprised of, persons who do not share the Court's view as to which words or expressions are acceptable and who, for a variety of reasons, including a conscious desire to flout majoritarian conventions, express themselves using words that may be regarded as offensive by those from different socio-economic backgrounds. In this context, the Court's decision may be seen for what, in the broader perspective, it really is: another of the dominant culture's inevitable efforts to force those groups who do not share its mores to conform to its way of thinking, acting, and speaking. . . .

Pacifica, in response to an FCC inquiry about its broadcast of Carlin's satire on "the words you couldn't say on the public airwaves," explained that "Carlin is not mouthing obscenities, he is merely using words to satirize as harmless and essentially silly our attitudes towards those words." . . . In confirming Carlin's prescience as a social commentator by the result it reaches today, the Court evinces an attitude towards the "seven dirty words" that many others besides Mr. Carlin and Pacifica might describe as "silly." Whether today's decision will similarly prove "harmless" remains to be seen. One can only hope that it will.

Cases Abridged or Cited

Index